CHANGING VISIONS

CHANGING VISIONS

Human Cognitive Maps:
Past, Present, and Future

Ervin Laszlo, Robert Artigiani
Allan Combs, Vilmos Csányi

Westport, Connecticut

Published in the United States and Canada by Praeger Publishers
88 Post Road West, Westport, CT 06881
An imprint of Greenwood Publishing Group, Inc.

Printed in the United States of America

The paper used in this book complies with the
Permanent Paper Standard issued by the National
Information Standards Organization (Z39.48–1984).

10 9 8 7 6 5 4 3 2 1

English language edition, except the United States and Canada,
published by Adamantine Press Limited, 3 Henrietta Street, Covent
Garden, London WC2E 8LU England.

First published in 1996

Library of Congress Cataloging-in-Publication Data

Changing visions : human cognitive maps : past, present, and future /
  Ervin Laszlo . . . [et al.] ; edited by Allan Combs.
      p.   cm.—(Praeger studies on the 21st century, ISSN
  1076–1850)
    Includes bibliographical references and index.
    ISBN 0–275–95676–8 (alk. paper)—ISBN 0–275–95677–6 (pbk. :
  alk. paper)
    1. Cognitive maps.   2. Cognitive maps—Social aspects.   3. Schemas
  (Psychology)   4. Human information processing.   5. Psychology,
  Comparative.   I. Laszlo, Ervin, 1932–   .   II. Combs, Allan, 1942–
  BF314.C43   1996
  153—dc20   96–15309

Library of Congress Catalog Card Number: 96–15309
ISBN: 0–275–95676–8   Cloth
      0–275–95677–6   Paperback

Copyright © 1996 by Adamantine Press Limited

Contents

Notes on the Authors

Professor Robert Artigiani teaches courses in the History and Philosophy of Science. A founding member of both the General Evolution Research Group and the Washington Evolutionary Systems Society (WESS), he is President of the editorial board of *World Futures: The Journal of General Evolution* and Vice President of WESS.

Professor Artigiani has lectured at many European, American, and Indian universities. He was among the first to perceive the social implications of contemporary scientific paradigms and has organized several conferences for discussing ways to reconcile the sciences and humanities.

He has published articles in several scholarly journals as well as in books edited by, among others, Ervin Laszlo.

Professor Allan Combs is a neuropsychologist and systems theorist at the University of North Carolina at Asheville and Saybrook Institute in San Francisco. Author of over fifty articles, chapters, and books on consciousness and the brain, he is co-founder of the Society for Chaos Theory in Psychology and a member of the General Evolution Research Group and the Club of Budapest.

His books include *Synchronicity: Science, Myth and the Trickster*, with Mark Holland; *Chaos Theory in Psychology and the Life Sciences*, edited with Robin Robertson; and *The Radiance of Being: Complexity, Chaos, and the Evolutions of Consciousness*.

Dr Combs has Psychology degrees from the Ohio State University and the University of Florida, and holds a doctorate in BioPsychology from the University of Georgia. He is Book Review Editor of the journal *World Futures*.

Vilmos Csányi is Professor of Ethology at the Lorand Eötvös, University of Budapest, Hungary, and the founder and Director of the Department of Ethology there. He is the author of more than one hundred research articles, twelve books, and many popular articles on various biological topics.

Ervin Laszlo, Ph.D. is editor of the journal *World Futures* and the author or editor of forty-nine books, including *The Choice* and *Goals for Human Society: A Report to the Club of Rome on the New Horizons of Global Community.*

Dr Laszlo was Professor of Philosophy at the State University of New York, and has taught Systems Science, Futures Studies, World Order Studies, and Aesthetics at Portland State University, the University of Houston, Princeton, and Indiana University.

As well as being President of the newly formed Club of Budapest and of the International Society for the Systems Sciences, he is a prominent member of the Club of Rome, and advisor to the Director-General of Unesco.

Introduction

Everybody carries a picture of the world in his head, said mathematician Henri Poincaré. Neither he, nor anyone else would add, however, that this picture must necessarily be correct. There is indeed such a thing as a "cognitive map" of the world we experience, but this map need not be a faithful representation of that world. Indeed, it is likely to be partial, and to contain illusory and mistaken elements. Faulty maps, however, prompt erroneous behaviors, giving rise to various kinds and degrees of shocks and surprises.

Shocks and surprises are not entirely avoidable, for the world is not knowable in its entirety (and, even if it were knowable in its entirety, it might still not be predictable in its entirety). However, beyond some margin of tolerance, shocks and surprises begin to eat into one's chances of well-being—even of survival. It is in everyone's interest, therefore, to make the picture that he or she carries in his or her head as faithful as possible to the world in which he or she actually lives.

Cognitive maps are held by individuals, but the set of cognitive maps of individuals produces a collective kind of construction that constitutes a *social* cognitive map. Such a map, once evolved, takes on a life of its own; it cannot be reduced or disaggregated to the particular maps held by individuals. Since we are guided both by our own individual cognitive map and by that of our society, attention must be paid to both. In this study we review the origins and development of individual and social cognitive maps.

The origin of cognitive maps in the animal kingdom provides a useful insight into the nature and function of the maps held by individuals, though it does not follow that human cognitive maps are nothing but animal maps in a refined form. The evolution of human cognitive maps in the course of history has further lessons: it shows how individuals interact with the cognitive maps of others in their historical time and place and evolve the map typical of their society. Reviewing the developmental background can help us better to understand our own situation here and now. The crucial question is how the cognitive maps held in our own brain–mind came about, and how they are being shaped today—above all, whether they are good enough to assure the goals of our own existence, and that of our peers.

Aside from such metaphysical questions as "is our map an assuredly true mapping of the reality that surrounds us?" we can ask more modest and pragmatic questions, such as "is our cognitive map faithful enough to the world around us to guide our steps without creating shocks and surprises that impair our well-being and threaten our survival?" Such questions are no longer matters of merely theoretical interest. We shall not survive either as individuals or as a species if our maps fail to reflect the nature of the world that surrounds us—a world with which we constantly interact and that, in some measure, we also create, albeit without necessarily recognizing what it is that we interact with and what it is that we create.

Making our own cognitive map an adequately faithful representation of the world around us does not require us to be scientists. Indeed, a scientist, being a specialist in a particular field, cannot help but have a narrow map, corresponding to his or her research specialty. Though such a map may be more exact than commonsense maps, it will not be of great assistance in guiding everyday behavior if it deals with nuclear processes on Gamma Centauri, or with any other topic typical of the highly focused attention of contemporary natural scientists. The human and social sciences, of course, come closer to promoting the formation of faithful maps of lived reality, but such maps may still be what psychologist Edward Tolman (1948) called "strip maps," rather than basically adequate representations. Religion, common sense, even art can fill in and sharpen one's world-picture, but only a realization that such pictures are fluid and adaptable, and come from many streams and dimensions of experiences can enable people constantly to update and adapt their cognitive maps and make them into functional guides for their action and behavior.

It is our hope that reviewing the origins, development, and current changes in individual and social cognitive maps will prompt the reader to become more conscious of the nature and role of his or her own map, and better able to adapt it to the exigencies of our changing world. The exercise, if undertaken with sincerity and attention, cannot but benefit both the individuals who undertake it and the human and social world in which they live.

CHAPTER ONE

The Cognitive Maps of Individuals

Cognitive maps are mental representations of the worlds in which we live. They are built of our individual experiences, recorded as memories and tested against the unceasing demands of reality. These maps, however, do not simply represent the worlds of our experience in a passive and unchanging way. They are, in fact, dynamic models of the environments in which we carry out our daily lives, and as such determine much of what we expect, and even what we see. Thus, they represent and at the same time participate in the creation of our individual realities. These ideas will be explored in the following pages, beginning with the creation of cognitive maps in the brain, then proceeding to the role of such maps in the creation of our experience of reality itself. From there we will move beyond the individual to the social fabric of reality, woven of individual cognitive maps, which ultimately form tapestries that have realities entirely of their own.

The idea of cognitive maps was developed in the early decades of this century by the American psychologist Edward Tolman (1886–1959). Like many psychologists of his day, he was interested in how laboratory rats learned to navigate mazes, but unlike his colleagues, he believed that the rats acquired a figural, or gestalt-like, knowledge of each entire maze. This amounted to a mental road map that the rat could use to find its way to food at the end of the run. Most psychologists of that era preferred more objective explanations of behavior, holding that rats simply learned to connect particular responses to particular stimuli. Tolman disagreed with this reductionistic view, according to which, in his words, the rats "helplessly" responded "to a succession of external stimuli—sights, sounds, smells, pressures, etc." (Tolman 1948: 190). He argued for the presence of internal representations of the environment that included parts of the maze well beyond what could be seen from any single location.

Many informal observations avowed the presence of cognitive maps. One rat, for instance, escaped from the start chamber and ran straight across the top of the maze to the finish box. In terms of systematic research, Tolman's most convincing demonstrations involved the process of *latent learning*. To demonstrate latent learning, the experimenter would place a rat in a maze and let it walk around and explore at leisure. No food or other reward was placed in the maze at this time. Later, however, when the same rat was trained to run the maze for food, it would perform better than a rat that did not have the benefit of previous experience with the maze. Evidently, in simply exploring the maze with no particular incentive to find its way through, the rat had learned something about the lay of the land. This learning was latent in the sense that it was not visible until the rat was later required to use the learning to find food. Tolman maintained that the rat had actually constructed an internal representation, a cognitive map, of the maze.

Tolman, of course, was interested in more than just rats, and intended the idea of cognitive maps to apply to other organisms as well, including human beings. Working with rats, however, he discovered that some cognitive maps are broad and comprehensive, while others, which he called "strip maps," are narrow and confining, causing the rat to restrict its searches to a small portion of the entire maze. He observed that strip maps can result from a number of factors, including too much training in a single runway, too few environmental cues, and strongly motivating or frustrating conditions. He felt that the latter produced what amounted to a state of anxiety, and believed that strip maps, or their equivalents in human beings, are at the root of many forms of behavioral pathology.

The Creation of Cognitive Maps

The extent to which the complex brain of the human being creates its own reality is a question that is still open (Anderson 1990). Among those who ponder such matters, all but a few agree that a substantial portion of our experience of "reality" is self-created. At the level of perception alone, it seems that the world does not simply present itself to us finished, as if our eyes were merely windows that allowed images to enter and pass on, unchanged, into the brain. As we move about in space, retinal images undergo fluid alterations in size, shape, brightness, and color that do not at all resemble the fixed landscapes we actually experience. The constancy of the perceived visual world bears witness to the active role played by the eye and the brain in interpreting the optical display that arrives at the retina. It seems that, as organisms, we are better suited to dealing with a universe of fixed and reliable properties than a more primary one of energy flux and transformation.

In recent years, the active role of the human in interpreting the raw data of the senses has come to be recognized as so profound that more than a few perceptual psychologists have found themselves tipping over into the field of cognitive psychology, which studies the active involvement of the mind in organizing and defining the world. One such psychologist is Ulric Neisser. In the 1960s, Neisser became interested in how retinal images are identified as familiar objects such as cups, shoes, airplanes, and pencils (Neisser 1976).

Neisser observed that a logical analysis of this problem suggests two general types of solution. One is that the brain acts like a computer, and sorts through all the objects represented in its memory to compare each with that represented in the retinal image. The search continues until a favorable match is obtained. This is called a *bottom-up* approach. Its computational cost, however, is enormous. The brain must be prepared to review virtually everything represented in its entire memory. In other words, it must check every known object against the one in front of it. Even for large computers such a task is too time-consuming to be practical unless the size of the search is artificially narrowed. The human brain, however, is not a computer but a biological organ. It is not designed to carry out multiple operations in the space of nanoseconds, and so is evidently not designed to enact computational programs that rely on speed for success.

The other type of solution is somehow to anticipate the type of object most likely to be represented by the retinal image, and then conduct a narrow search within the anticipated category. This strategy, termed a *top-down* approach, still requires some searching, but narrows it to the objects most likely to be seen. Suppose, for instance, that one sees an object on the kitchen counter. Here, the context of the kitchen immediately narrows the search to objects such as a butter knife, can opener, or pie pan. Such objects will be more quickly recognized than a screwdriver or a pipe wrench. The bottom-up approach requires that the brain (or computer) have a certain amount of knowledge about how the world works, in this case about what kinds of object are commonly found in various locations about the house, in kitchens, workshops, bathrooms, and so forth. Neisser called such patterns of information *anticipatory schemata.*

Based on such considerations and the results of much research,

Neisser developed the *perceptual cycle* model, according to which activity moves, or cycles, between these two modes. Confronted with an object on the kitchen counter, a pipe wrench for instance, one would first expect it to be something commonly found in the kitchen. Failing to recognize the object, one momentarily flounders before entertaining comparisons from other schemata, such as the one that identifies objects found in the bathroom or workshop.

All of this, of course, concerns the act of recognition. However, the ability of the eye and brain to produce a solid visual experience despite the continuous fluctuation of the retinal image hints at a deeper enigma. This is the question of how, out of the mercurial flux of energies that continually rain down on the sensory organs of the body, the nervous system constructs the experience of a solid world in the first place. And beyond this, to what extent, if any, does that construction represent some "real," objective world beyond the senses?

In a classic study of the evolution of the nervous system, Jerison (1973) showed that one of the brain's central problems is to coordinate sensory input as it arrives on a number of diverse channels—touch, taste, smell, hearing, and vision. He pointed out that the most efficient mechanism for bringing about a complete integration of these disparate channels is to project—in a word, *create*—a unified external reality within which sensory features can be located. It is easier for the brain to deal with a solid living tiger than to consider separately the implications of its odor, its stripes, its roar, and so on!

Jerison argued that the mode of sensory integration developed by mammals is essentially visual. Its beginnings go back to the late Triassic period, about 200 million years ago, when mammals first appeared as nocturnal "reptiles" in whom audition came to replace vision as the primary distance sense. Neurologically, the transition from vision to audition was accomplished by the remapping of auditory input onto previously established reptilian visual networks, which, like the retina itself, represented vision in a spatially distributed fashion. In time, the mammalian forebrain became the center in which virtually all the external senses are mapped into a visually structured world. Thus the mammalian brain became a world-maker. In Jerison's words:

"Reality" or a "real world" is a construction of the nervous system. It is, in fact, a model of a possible world which enables the nervous system to process the mass of incoming and outgoing information in a consistent way. It is a trick, as it were, to enable an organism with a large nervous system to handle almost inconceivably large amounts of information that are usually thought of as nerve impulses or states of membranes of single cells. (1973: 410)

In other words, from a neurologically informed perspective, the experienced world is a map.

It is of interest that recent research has provided substantial support for an understanding of the brain that views it as taking in frequency information—sound frequency, visuospatial frequency, and so on—and, by processes analogous to those of holography, using this information to create a unified perceptual world (Globus 1987a; Pribram 1991).

Just how much flexibility is allowed in this process of world formation is anyone's guess (Anderson 1990). It is apparent from both anthropology and history that different cultures have survived admirably well using widely disparate maps of reality. On the other hand, a visit to the local psychiatric hospital, or an attempt to build a simple electric circuit at home, will demonstrate that there are limits to improvisation.

At the most conservative extreme, the prominent psychologist J. J. Gibson started a school of perceptual psychology that champions the idea that the visual display arriving at the eye carries pre-packaged within itself all the relationships that characterize external reality (Gibson 1966). These are simply picked up, or at best interpreted, and there is no need for internal representations along the lines of a cognitive map—certainly not at the sensory level. Such realism, however, is considered a little naive by most scientists. At the other extreme neuropsychiatrist Gordon Globus (1987a) argues that, in its enormous complexity and flexibility, the human brain is capable of creating and projecting a virtually unlimited number of entire worlds. He states that "the brain in its unsurpassed complexity generates its own holoplenum of *possibilia*—a virtual holoworld of possible worlds" (p. 378). From the evidence of altered states of consciousness, shamanism, and the experience of ordinary dreams, he concludes that "human beings have the capacity to constitute *de novo* perfectly authentic worlds . . . worlds which have never previously been experienced" (p. 382). Surely the answer falls somewhere between the poles represented by these two opinions. It is certain, however, that if we do not create the universe *ex nihilo*, we actively participate in molding our experience of it.

A startling observation that emerges from all of the above is that the maps that the nervous system spins of reality are, for the person concerned, no less than reality itself. In a sense that is not trivial—and contrary to the famous words of Count Alfred Korzybski (1958)—the map *is* the territory. What is more, such mapmaking (reality-spinning) is not limited to sensory perception, but extends to virtually all levels of experience. Not only do we see the pipe wrench on the kitchen counter as a solid object with fixed features—despite fluctuations in lighting, distance, and angle subtended at the eye—but the fact that it presents itself to us as a pipe wrench and not a hammer, paperweight, tomahawk, or the jawbone of a god, that it is owned by a particular person and is not communal property, and that it is out of place in the kitchen, all attest to the character of the cognitive maps (reality) by which we appraise it.

It seems that maintaining highly consistent cognitive maps is a passion, indeed an obsession, of human beings. Neuropsychologist Michael Gazzaniga (1985) has in fact postulated the existence of a left-hemispheric brain process called the *interpreter*, the job of which is to monitor everything coming out of other brain processes, such as those concerned with memory, emotion, and the senses, in order to come up with a coherent picture (map) of the individual's immediate situation. It might observe, for instance, "My memory tells me that I haven't eaten for several hours, I notice that my stomach feels hollow and that my mouth is watering, and I am experiencing fantasies of food. I interpret all this to mean I am hungry." This example is too literal because it assumes the interpreter to be conscious of its own operation—and apparently it is not—but it captures the basic idea of how it works.

The dramatic thing about this interpreter is that it seems impelled to conceive a single interpretation of reality, a unitary mapping of the events of the moment, and then stick to it tenaciously, even when the product is patently distorted. For example, Gazzaniga (1985) tells of a woman who was hospitalized at the Memorial Sloan-Kettering hospital in New York City with damage to her right parietal lobe. She was charming, witty, and in all ways intelligent, except that she insisted she was at her home in Freeport, Maine! No one could convince her otherwise. In desperation, Gazzaniga pointed to the big hospital elevator doors just outside her room and asked, "What are those things over there?" "Those," she responded, "are elevators. Do you have any idea what it cost me to have them put in my house?"

According to Gazzaniga, the problem with this woman was that whatever brain mechanism is responsible for keeping track of real-time location was producing dramatically distorted output, while other brain systems continued to function as usual, oblivious to the error. It seemed simply to be beyond the capability of this otherwise intelligent woman to recognize the distortion in her map that located her in Freeport, Maine.

It would appear that as human beings each of us stands at the center of a multitude of self-created maps of reality, each of which charts some dimension of our experience. Some maps, such as the one gone wrong for the lady in the Memorial Sloan-Kettering hospital, graph our physical landscapes, plotting our location and movement in space and time. Others map overlapping classes of information useful in different spheres of our daily lives, while still others chart value systems. The class of information needed to visit a restaurant, for instance, includes rules for how to interact with the waiter and the maître d', when and where to leave the tip, how to eat in a mannerly fashion, and so on. These rules, of course, differ somewhat from restaurant to restaurant, depending on variables such as social class and ethnic orientation. Since classes of information such as that needed for proper restaurant behavior seem to form recognizable patterns, they are often understood by cognitive scientists as *schemata*, not unlike Neisser's perceptual schemata, which provided information about a particular visual situation. These terms are similar to our use of the term *map*.

Such maps, or schemata, turn out to be surprisingly complex. A couple of decades ago, when artificial intelligence experts first began to program computers to simulate simple human behaviors, it was discovered, much to the consternation of the programmers, that without exquisitely elaborate programs, computers made unbelievably stupid errors. A simulation of a restaurant scene, for instance, might find the patrons entering by walking directly through the walls, whereupon they might seat themselves on the floor (exactly where the computer probably has the waiter serve the food) and eventually tip the cook before leaving. To get this scene right, the programmer must supply the computer with an enormous amount of commonsense information of the kind that makes up the basic cognitive maps that guide human behavior.

The human "restaurant map," as we will call it, overlaps with larger maps that represent general rules for how to behave in public. If we know these larger maps well, we are unlikely to go too far afield in our restaurant behavior. Maps that carry information about our professions, as well those that govern our relationships with members of our immediate families, are more general than the restaurant map. On the other hand, they are more limited than those governing public behavior in general. Moreover, the information contained in these various maps is highly redundant. Thus, it is perhaps not surprising that damage to particular regions of the brain rarely destroys entire cognitive maps. Brain injury patients rarely loose their entire sense of social protocol, or their entire knowledge of where things are in space. On the other hand, more limited maps are vulnerable. Thus, we read of seemingly bizarre cases in which a stroke victim has lost his ability to recall the names of garden flowers, say, or vegetables.

The notion of maps, like that of schemata, implies a connected world of experience. Maps can vary in breadth as well as in detail. Among cartographers there is the further understanding that each map utilizes some particular *projection*, or coordinate system, that is laid out in a specific fashion. Flat maps representing the sphere of the Earth, for instance, have strikingly different appearances depending on the nature of the projection used. If the metaphor of projections can be carried over to cognitive maps, then different projection systems would be equivalent to different ways of organizing reality. Here we are not speaking of the actual content displayed by the maps. Rather, it is a matter of how the content is represented. All projections of the Earth exhibit the same continents, but their appearance differs according to the nature of the projection. The bottom line is that each projection system is the equivalent of a unique experienced world.

Cognitive Maps in Animals

Before proceeding further in our examination of cognitive maps in humans, let us trace the origins of cognitive maps in the animal kingdom. This will provide us with a wider perspective from which to further our understanding of cognitive maps. Animals have developed such organs as the nervous system and the brain for perceiving, understanding, and influencing the external world in the interests of their own survival. But the brains of animals can never grasp the surrounding world in its totality. They focus, rather, on those aspects of the environment that are essential for their own survival and reproduction. We will refer to these aspects as *environmental information.*

Information about the environment influences animals in at least two ways. On the one hand it affects their immediate behavior. On the other hand—and this is equally important—it takes part in events leading to the evolution of entirely new behavior patterns.

Every animal species has a special food-acquiring behavior pattern. The blue tit, for example, searches for insects in the cracks of bark on trees—an activity that presupposes an appropriate bill, good sight, and a brain that is able to process the perceived stimuli very quickly. The techniques for acquiring food can be very sophisticated, including the use of traps, radio-location, electricity, and an extremely refined mind. The food-getting activities of animals are controlled by the best kind of "computer" in the world, the nervous system. In lower invertebrates, the nervous system is only slightly "programmable," so these kinds of animal do not learn much during their life. The technique for acquiring their food is a genetic heritage, stored in the "genetic memory." The way spiders spin nets or catch and kill their prey is entirely determined by genetic programs.

If a food-getting technique were analyzed in order to find the simplest units of behavioral instruction (called algorithms in computer language), we would find these algorithms stored mainly in genetic memory. In the course of its development, the animal's nervous system has been programmed for the proper algorithms by the genetic memory. Whenever it is necessary, the programs are activated automatically by information from the environment and the animal fulfills these instructions exactly. Instructions are not rigid; they are able to evolve. Natural selection ensures that the behavioral algorithms are always nearly perfect. For example, if a spider is born without the ability to spin nets, owing to some genetic or developmental defect, it will not be able to catch its food and, therefore, to produce offspring. Thus the wrong program cannot be transmitted to the next generation. However, occasionally a slight transformation of the original program in the genetic material slightly improves the behavioral algorithm. In this case, the transformation can survive in the offspring and it is this which forms the basis for the evolution of behavior. As a consequence of natural selection, the food-getting behavior of an animal is exactly that which enables it to obtain food within the natural environment.

The higher vertebrates are not only supported by their genetic memory—although a great variety of instructions are also fixed in it—but are also provided with a neural memory, developed during the course of various learning processes and permitting a more sophisticated adaptation compared to the genetic memory. Mammals, particularly, have a highly developed memory of this kind, as the young benefit from a long period of parental guidance—something that provides the opportunity for the young to acquire the most appropriate behavioral algorithms. The two kinds of memory are not separated rigorously but combine subtly during the life of the animal. Predatory mammals hold instructions in their genetic memory such as "chase everything that moves." This is a general instruction and we can observe it very well in the behavior of juvenile predators. As soon as they are able to move, they chase any moving object, including their litter-mates, their mother (or her tail), fallen leaves whirled along by the wind, but mostly any living creatures that move. The special function of neural memory is to make the general instruction more specific, to "fill it up" according to the actual life-circumstances of the animal, which must realize that not every moving object represents prey. In the course of the fine-tuning of the neural memory, the animal has many chances to learn mechanisms used by its own parents, or it can discover new tricks for acquiring food more efficiently.

All of the special mechanisms of the nervous system serve to acquire relevant information, interpreted to the animal's own benefit. In other words, the nervous system acts like a huge filter, neglecting and ex-cluding effects that are presumably not needed by the animal. There-fore, the world which is seen, heard, or perceived by animals differs widely from the (presumed) real one. From the external environment, the animals are affected continuously by various events. Some of these events—which we call *stimuli*—have special importance regarding the survival of the animals, but others do not. Only environmental factors that influence the nervous system become information perceived by the receptors. This further narrows the set of stimuli processed by the brain. It is very important, therefore, for all animals to respond only to essential aspects of their environment. Their nervous systems have the ability to choose the aspects to be responded to. Different mechanisms of the nervous system serve this function; some of them do so by way of the receptors of the sense organs (these are the sensory stimulus-filters), while others influence central information-processing (the central stimulus-filters).

Some kind of stimulus-filtering is provided by various sense organs as a result of the limits of their sensitivity and capacity. The human ear cannot hear sounds above a frequency of 20 kilohertz and the human eye cannot see ultraviolet and infrared light waves, whereas certain other animals can perceive these very well. An interesting example of the selectivity of sense organs was discovered in a tree frog (*Eleuthero-dactylus coqui*). This frog was named after the male's characteristic croaking, which sounds something like "co-qui." The male's croaking frightens other males but is attractive to females. The reason is that the males perceive only the "co" sound from the whole croaking, while the females perceive only the "qui" calling them. The basis of this selectivity is the different tuning of the ear membrane in the male and female frogs (McFarland 1985).

Frog vision is restricted in a special way by the receptor cells of the retina, as has been shown in the leopard frog (*Rana pipiens*). H. R. Maturana and his co-workers (1960) detected five kinds of sensory neuron in the retina of the frog, which fire when receiving quite different stimuli. One of these types is stimulated if the light is switched on or off, or if the illumination is decreasing or increasing. This type will fire if an object passes through the field of vision, but only in cases where the edge of the object is within the field of the given neuron. (There is normally no reaction to an object that is constantly present in the visual field, except when the object's illumination changes.) This type of neuron is called a contrast-detector. The second type, not sensitive to changes in illumination but reacting to passing clear edges, is called a contour-detector. The third type reacts to decreasing illumination independently of any motion; the fourth type reacts when illumination increases. These receptors continuously measure the increase or decrease in light intensity. But the most interesting is the fifth type of neuron, which Maturana called a bug-detector. This type begins to fire with great intensity if a small (compared to the visual field) and dark (compared to the background) object crosses the visual field. The retina of the frog represents a very effective filter mechanism; any information reaching the brain is already selected according to the subsequent actions of feeding or flight. In the first case, a small object moves, which could be snatched and swallowed; in the other case, there is a big and dark object that it is better to avoid.

Some moth species from the genus *Catocala*, which are hunted by bats, have a special "ear," the so-called *tympanal organ*. This consists of a membrane that is able to oscillate and a small air pocket behind it (Roeder and Treat 1961). The oscillations of the membrane are sensed by neurons and transmitted to the moth's central nervous system. Using the tympanal organ, the moth is able to detect the ultrasound of approaching bats and tries to avoid them with the appropriate movements. Based on Roeder and Treat's studies we know that significant stimulus-filtering occurs in the tympanal organ. Thin electrodes were implanted into the axons of the two types of neuron (A1, A2) that are in contact with the tympanal membrane to investigate how each type reacts when different kinds of sound are generated near the moth. It turned out that neither of the neurons reacts specifically to the frequency of the sounds, which indicates that the moths are unable to detect the bats by this means. In fact, it is the intensity of the sounds that is of real importance; if it is low, only the A1 neurons fire, but if the sounds are strong both A1 and A2 neurons start firing and, additionally, the rate of A1 firing increases significantly. Thus, of the various sound parameters reaching the moth during flight, the nervous system is interested solely in the perception of the intensity of the sounds. This peculiar behavior of the two kinds of neuron provides the moth with sufficient information to survive. The limits of perception are ensured by genetic factors.

Generally speaking, insects look at, listen to, smell, or taste only that which is especially important for them, while higher animals usually have less selective, more universal sensors. For example, humans can distinguish a large variety of odors because the olfactory receptors are not highly specific. On the other hand, the male silk moth shows a very specific and sensitive reaction to a single scent compound, bombykol, secreted by a special abdominal gland in the female. The male is able to perceive this scent even if the female is several kilometers away because the neurons of the olfactory receptors begin to fire as soon as a single molecule of bombykol reaches a sensory cell (Payne 1974). This is the maximum sensitivity that is theoretically possible. However, these receptors do not show any reaction to other scents.

It is not only the particular selectivity of the sense organs that acts as a filter on the environmental effects recognized by animals; there is also an efficient processing of information in the central nervous system directed by genetic memory. The two important ethological concepts concerning the central stimulus-filters are the key-stimulus and the releasing mechanism. Lack (1939) was the first to observe that male robins (*Erithacus rubecula*) attack other males of the same species that have red feathers on their breast if they happen to enter their territory during the breeding period. The birds also vigorously attack a stuffed robin, but only if it has red feathers on its breast. A stuffed bird with the red feathers painted black is ignored. Lack also showed that robins even attack a bunch of red feathers as if these were another aggressive male. The conclusion is unambiguous: territorial defense is triggered by the sight of red feathers in spite of the fact that the bird is apparently able to perceive other features of the species members. Thus, the filtering of stimuli is not performed by the sensory receptors but is based on a central processing of information; that is, a central selection occurs. Stimuli playing a role in situations such as the above are called *key-stimuli* in ethology.

Key-stimuli may also change according to the internal state of the animal. The herring gull (*Larus argentatus*) often steals and eats the eggs of other birds nesting in the same colony. It has been shown by Tinbergen (1960) that when stealing eggs the gull recognizes them according to their shape, but when its own eggs roll out of the nest, their size and color pattern become the key-stimuli, and it pulls them back with characteristic movements. However, when it returns to the eggs to continue brooding, shape becomes significant again through tactile sensation. If the pulled-in objects are not round it does not remain sitting on them. Thus, the gull's egg, through three different groups of stimuli, activates three different actions (Tinbergen 1960). Based on these and similar events, it is possible to make a distinction between perceived stimuli (acting on the receptors and activating them) and effective stimuli (triggering a typical activity).

Another animal that demonstrates this difference is the diving beetle. The beetle often hunts tadpoles, but if a tadpole is placed in a glass tube, the diving beetle will not try to catch it. On the other hand, it will chase a plug of cotton wool wildly if there is a tiny piece of meat inside. This means that the triggering key-stimulus for capturing behavior is of a chemical nature (Eibl-Eibesfeldt 1970).

The female turkey recognizes her chicks by their sound, and can be made to brood a stuffed polecat if turkey-chick peeping is heard through a tiny loud-speaker inside. If a brooding turkey has been deafened before the first hatching, she will kill her chicks because she does not hear the sounds. However, if the mother turkey has already had a chance to brood before the operation, she will accept her chicks in spite of her deafness (Schleidt, Schleidt, and Magg 1960). This means that, through learning, visual stimuli might be substituted for the important key-stimulus, sound. Thus, in some cases, genetic and neural memories can substitute for one another.

Ethologists assume that there is a central, innate releasing mechanism (RM) belonging to each of the key-stimuli, a special part of the nervous system where the key-stimulus is recognized and a behavioral instruction is initiated to perform the proper reaction. It was also originally supposed that in the absence of the key-stimulus (also called a *releaser*), responses are inhibited by the releasing mechanism; that is, the neural action-centers are always ready to fire but the specific RMs inhibit their manifestation. In fact, it turned out that the early theory of RMs is not as generally applicable as was supposed. Although in many cases it has been possible to demonstrate the existence of RMs by neurophysiological experiments, in other cases it has become clear that the responses given to particular stimuli emerge from the interaction of different parts of the brain. Whatever the correct description, the model of key-stimulus and releasing mechanism is a current and important explanatory idea in ethology.

The key-stimulus is often complex, and the real releaser is a particular relationship between the stimulus components. This type of key-stimulus is called a *configurational stimulus*. The young of the blackbird (*Turdus merula*) perform an intense gaping reaction when presented with even a very simplified dummy of the adult bird, consisting of two connected black disks, differing in size. The young gape in the direction of the smaller disk as if it were the head of a parent. In this case the key-stimulus is the size relation of the two disks. If a "two-headed" dummy is shown, the young gape at only one of the heads, chosen on the basis of the size relations (Eibl-Eibesfeldt 1970).

It often happens that the same behavior is elicited by several, different key-stimuli, the effects of which are more or less additive. The red abdomen of male sticklebacks elicits aggression in other males of the same species. During fighting, the males keep themselves in a per-pendicular position, "standing on their head," because the head-down position is also a strong key-stimulus that triggers fighting. If a territory-seeking male is presented with a dummy of a stickleback, it will accept only these two key-stimuli. The most intensive attack can be triggered by a red-bellied dummy in the head-down position, although a red-throated model induces some fighting even in the hori-zontal position. A dummy not painted at all elicits some reaction only in the head-down position. This kind of additive effect of key-stimuli is called the *rule of heterogeneous summation*, described by Seitz (1940).

In the case of many animals, the key-stimulus comprises two compo-nents, a defined shape and a motion pattern. The males of wolf spiders and of fiddler crabs display characteristic waving movements of their specialized forelimbs when approaching females. The shape and the movement of the forelimb combined represent the key-stimulus that inhibits aggressive behavior by the females. Many key-stimuli similar to this operate in birds, too. They are referred to as *sign stimuli* in current scientific terminology.

Beside key-stimuli, the *search image* represents another important mechanism for connecting the animal with its environment. While recognition of key-stimuli is determined by genetic memory, the mech-anism of the search image is based on neural memory. Many people have probably experienced not noticing an object they were searching excitedly for although it was right under their nose, but not exactly in the form imagined. Uexkuell (1934) described how he was searching for a water jug on the table, a clay one, but did not notice it standing right in front of him because it was made of glass. In analyzing his own experience he named the engram recalled from memory during the searching process a search image. The search image controls the action of the brain while looking for a given object. For instance, if we are looking for a name in a book it is not necessary to read letter by letter; it is enough just to scan the pages, "searching" for the given word picture. A trained person has usually only to glance at a page to be able to decide with considerable certainty whether a given name is on that page or not.

Based on Uexkuell's many other observations it is most probable that the animal brain also makes use of search images. He observed, for example, that, if he fed a hungry toad an earthworm, during the next minutes the animal was inclined to snap at any long, worm-like object. But if the toad ate a spider first, it would be more inclined to snap at ants or insect-like objects. If a finch or a jay catches a caterpillar imitating a little branch, for a period of time it will be inclined to peck at twigs similar to the caterpillar.

Cowie, Krebs, and Sherry (1981) investigated how the hunting of insects by tits depends on the availability of different insect species. They discovered that if tits are provided with various but rarely occurring insects, then they hunt randomly. If the number of individuals of one of the insect species increases above a well-defined encounter rate, the tits begin to eat more of this species than would be theoretically expected. Tits become "accustomed" to hunting the species spread abundantly and to neglecting others. If in the meantime the number of the preferred species decreases, the tits continue to gather them for a while even though it is no longer economical. As time passes, they encounter this species only rarely, and begin to hunt another species. This behavior can also be explained by the development of a search image. While the tits are prepared to hunt for a variety of insects, a search image cannot be formed, but if members of a given species are encountered more frequently, a search image will develop based on memory. It helps the animal to concentrate on perceptual patterns similar to the object searched for, and this considerably increases efficiency.

In field experiments with crows, Croze (1970) demonstrated the development of the search image. Over a relatively large area on a seashore, he placed empty shells painted in different colors. He hid pieces of meat under differently colored shells at different rates. It was observed that when the crows arrived they first turned up each of the colorful red, blue, and yellow shells, one after the other. If one of the colors signaled food more frequently than the others, they began to search over the whole area but turned up only shells of the color under which they had found most food before. This behavior can also be explained by the development of a search image, and shows simultaneously how efficient behavior can be. The crows did not waste their time and energy by investigating seemingly hopeless varieties of shell.

Although the search image can serve in the short term, I. S.

Beritashvili, a Georgian neurophysiologist, discovered *image memory*, which has a different function. Beritashvili (1971) studied a variety of vertebrates ranging from fish to chimpanzees. The experimental protocol was usually the following: a food source was shown to the animal under investigation for a short time, although the animal was not permitted to get to the food immediately but only after some time had passed. It was then noted whether it tried to go directly to where it had seen the food before, or whether it searched at random. From the behavior of the animal it was possible to determine how long it remembered the position of the food. With fish, the investigation was performed in an aquarium divided into several compartments. The hungry fish was placed into a start-box, and a piece of food in one of the other boxes. The fish was then cautiously directed, using a net, to the box where it could eat the food. After feeding, the fish was placed back into the start-box. In the beginning the fish were frightened by this process, but they gradually became accustomed to it, and when the door of the start-box was opened, they swam out voluntarily. According to Beritashvili, the fish were able to remember the box where they had been fed for approximately ten seconds. If the time between feeding and the return to the start-box was less than ten seconds, the fish found their way back to the box where they had been fed before. If the time was longer, they swam at random or went mostly to the central compartment.

Beritashvili conducted similar experiments with frogs. They were able to remember for several minutes which box had previously contained food. This was also the approximate time limit for turtles. In an experiment with pigeons it was found that they could remember the location of food shown once, for two to three minutes. However, if they were permitted to go there and even eat some grains, the time increased considerably and the pigeons remembered the location of the food for several days.

Beritashvili also performed experiments with mammals, mostly dogs. One such experiment was conducted in a large room where the dog was placed in a cage. From behind one of several wooden screens in the room the experimenter showed a bowl containing food and drew the attention of the animal to it. Sometimes the experimenter not only showed the food but also gave sound signals, by tapping the bottom of the bowl, for example. In other experiments the animal was led to the screen and allowed to sniff at the food, and occasionally to eat some pieces. After this the animal was left alone for a given time in the cage. When the dog was allowed to come out again, Beritashvili observed how it tried to find the food, which had been hidden behind the screen again. The experiments demonstrated that the dog would immediately run to the proper place, even after about two hours, and even when the food had been shown only from a distance. If more than two hours passed between showing and releasing, the dog would remember the food as something that "had to be somewhere in the room" but it would have forgotten the exact place and would run around searching at random. The image memory increased strongly, however, if the dog had been allowed to go to the place and to eat some pieces. In this situation the dog would hurry immediately to the proper screen, even after eighteen days. Of course, in these long-term experiments, the waiting time was not spent in the room.

Beritashvili found the memory of baboons to be even better: they remembered the exact position of food behind the screens even after six weeks, provided they had eaten there before.

These observations are of great value to us because they show what an important role a picture stored in memory can play in the regulation of animal behavior. Following its formation, the picture may be effective for hours, days, or even weeks (the duration is important because it clearly distinguishes between image memory and the search image; the latter is a short-term memory trace formed during searching). We must emphasize the importance of these findings, since other experiments on conditioned reflexes or operant conditioning have mainly concentrated on direct responses elicited by stimuli. The animals have been treated as a reflex machine from which an external stimulus can always elicit some response. The most important consequence of the experiments of Beritashvili is that it is the internal representation of the stimulus that influences the animal, and that this effect may last for a long time independently of the external environment.

Beside the search image and the image memory, we know of other mechanisms of the nervous system, also connected with memory, that are used for orientation within an animal's close surroundings. Even insects make use of these, despite the fact that their behavior is mainly directed by rigid rules fixed in genetic memory. Many insects return to the same location repeatedly for a special purpose, in which case it is the neural memory that directs their orientation. When a bee leaves the hive, it can be seen to fly some exploratory circles around the hive. It has been shown experimentally that, during this flight, it memorizes larger, conspicuous objects, like trees and houses, surrounding the hive. Is some form of "representation" of the environment formed in the brain of the bee or other insects that is able to orient them?

An earlier study by Tinbergen (1932) dealt with this kind of learning in the case of the digger wasp (*Philanthus triangulum*). The female digger wasp digs a burrow in the soft sand and supplies her growing larvae daily with immobilized bees, which are her special prey. Tinbergen and Kruy (1938) demonstrated that before flying off the wasp makes an "orienting flight" for some seconds in the vicinity of her burrow, during which she stores the characteristic points of the area in her memory. When she comes back after some hours with prey, her memory helps her to find the burrow. In the course of experiments for his 1932 paper, Tinbergen marked the burrow while the wasp was inside, ringing the exit with twenty pine cones. After the wasp had flown off, he placed all of the cones in the same arrangement but further away, at a distance of about 30 cm from the hole. The wasp now sought her burrow at the center of the cone ring but failed to find it until the original situation was restored. Beusekom (1946) has shown that the digger wasp uses several orienting cues simultaneously. In one of the experiments, he marked the burrow using a wooden cube and a shrub twig. When he moved the cube and turned it by 45 degrees before the wasp returned, the insect sought the entrance of her burrow according to the actual position of the twig. We can conclude from this and similar experiments that the wasp fixes a visual pattern in her memory and also fixes the position of the burrow in relation to this pattern. The more an object stands out from the surroundings, the more important is its contribution to the pattern. Consequently, certain elements or features of the pattern are selected by the animal's senses based on genetic memory, while their representation is later transferred to neural memory. The nervous system makes a comparison between the memory pattern and the actual perceptual pattern. (In principle, the innate releasing mechanism works similarly, but in the case of stimulus patterns formed in memory under the influence of the environment, they are compared by the brain to the pattern of key-stimuli in the genetic memory.)

Orientation, supported by external stimulus patterns, is used actively by most animals who seek to return to the nest or home. Of course, they need not only the stimulus pattern of their destination but also stimuli that help them find each step of the way back. Therefore external stimulus patterns must overlap each other. When an animal is placed in a new surroundings it can often be observed to return repeatedly to the point where it was first placed, using it as a starting base for the exploration of the new environment. Gradually it forms the memory patterns necessary for its proper orientation.

Higher animals not only have to orient themselves in their natural environment if they are to survive, they must also be ready to escape the attacks of their enemies, to obtain food and shelter, to take care of their offspring—and all of these in a permanently changing world. Everything changes in the local environment: enemies, possibilities of obtaining food and even the most elementary physical conditions change with the change of the seasons. Consequently, higher animals must solve complex tasks that utilize their various capabilities simultaneously.

The cognitive maps of these animals are extremely complex and must be of a rather dynamic, continuously changing nature. A very large part of an animal's activity is devoted to constructing cognitive maps. Emil Menzel (1978) performed experiments with juvenile, 3-year-old chimpanzees in order to study the formation of dynamic cognitive maps. The "environment" consisted of a 0.4 hectare bushy, grassy enclosure with several trees in the middle. In a preliminary experiment, the animals were transported in cages to the margins of the area and released daily for one or two hours. Their behavior was registered from an observation tower and analyzed in detail. On entering the new place the animals became very excited. They first examined the whole area and then occupied a central position, which allowed them to observe the area in all directions. Using these places as "headquarters," the apes began systematically to explore the whole area in detail. This activity lasted several weeks, and the main experiment was begun when the animals had finished it.

The experimenters added twenty different toys and household utensils (durable enough to resist the intense interest of the chimpanzees) to the numerous other objects found on the ground. The animals became acquainted with the new objects during the 30-minute daily sessions run every second day (the total duration of these sessions was 5 hours). The 10-day period of familiarization was followed by a 10-day testing period, with daily sessions of 30 minutes. On each of these days, an additional new object was placed among the others. Thus, on the eleventh day of the experiment, twenty-one objects could be found in the area, while on day twenty, there were thirty. During the first five days the newest objects were placed in a separate location from the former; during the next five days they were placed among the older objects. Thus, the effect of both the new object and the new location could be observed. Finally, some older objects were removed and the position of other objects was changed.

The chimps noticed each new object immediately, and went to it and examined it carefully within 15 seconds of their entry into the experimental area. Finding an old object in a new place also provoked a little interest, but the object was investigated only briefly. Other experiments also demonstrated that chimpanzees remember very precisely the location of objects for weeks. As was pointed out by Menzel, their capabilities are not inferior to the corresponding ones in humans. Field observations have demonstrated that chimpanzees know their environment in great detail. The dynamic cognitive map formed in their brain could instead be considered a cognitive model, as it contains not only a map of the physical environment but also the changes and the possible alternatives.

Based on similar observations, a new concept regarding the role of the brain has emerged. According to this concept, the main function of the brain is the formation of a dynamic model of the environment. The chimp's brain, with its huge memorizing capacity, is able to represent surrounding objects and places exactly, and to register changes minute by minute. Thus, the chimp's environmental model is "up to date" at all times.

The Neurological Basis of Cognitive Maps

Of course, we know of the existence of cognitive maps not only from ethological and psychological experiments but also from neurological investigations. With the help of micro-electrodes implanted into the brain, it is possible to map which neurons respond to particular stimuli affecting the animal, and how these are arranged within the perceptual areas of the brain. Through the investigation of mammalian hearing, it has been shown that in the auditory cortex, large and quite specific neurons can be found that fire only if the animal hears a specific sound from an extremely narrow frequency range (e.g. Uttal 1973). At the same time, other, more broadly tuned neurons cover the whole frequency range. The sound-detector neurons are arranged alongside each other on the surface of the brain according to the frequency ranges. Similar arrangements are quite common in the nervous systems of higher animals. For example, in the visual cortex, we find a topographical map of the retina's receptors with each neuron responding to stimuli coming from a given segment of the visual field. Since the cortex of the brain processes the two-dimensional picture on the retina in various ways (according to the direction of movement, the angles between edges compared to each other, and so forth), it seems to be most convenient for processing if the receptor neurons of the brain accurately represent the spatial localization of the receptor cells of the retina. In this case we have an example of the physical realization of a cognitive map.

In the examples above, the central nervous system "transcribes" the two-dimensional stimulus patterns arriving at the sensory surface onto the neuron networks of the brain. One explanation for this might be that it is the simplest way to organize the processing of two-dimensional patterns during development. In recent years, however, it has been shown that a spatial representation of the environment is present in the central nervous system in an analogous form, even if the sense organs do not produce a two-dimensional pattern. Thus a "real" model of the environment is formed. The hearing of owls is very refined, since this is their most important sense for locating prey. There is a region in the owl's midbrain in which a precise spatial representation of the direction of sounds, similar to the neural representation of visual images in mammals, can be found, even though the owl's ears are not stimulated by a sound pattern arranged spatially, but rather by a sequence of sounds (Knudsen 1981). Each neuron in this cognitive map responds to sounds coming from a particular location, so that the different neurons are "listening" to different spatial areas. Whereas in vision the position of a stimulus is determined by the horizontal and vertical coordinates of the retina, in hearing the direction of a sound is determined by comparing the times of arrival and the intensities at the two ears. This makes it possible to create a three-dimensional map of the sources of the sounds. In the case of the owl, about half of the brain region processing sound maps is devoted to an area of 15 degrees just in front of the owl, which represents the most sensitive area for spatial hearing. Also, the area of the owl's brain that processes sounds coming from below is larger than the area that processes those coming from above. From the predatory viewpoint of the owl the information coming from below is more important.

A similarly elegant example of the physical existence of cognitive maps is provided by electrophysiological investigations of the auditory cortex of bats (Suga, Kuzirai, and O'Neil 1981). A model of the physical environment is constructed by analyzing the echoes from the ultrasounds that bats emit. Thus, those parts of the bat's brain that analyze sounds are considerably enlarged in comparison with other animals. The auditory cortex can be divided into several parts with different physiological functions. These provide important information about insect prey crossing the bat's path. Separate regions are concerned with the distance, size, relative velocity, and the wing-beat frequency of the prey (the latter helps to identify it). From the delay between the emission and the echo of the orientation pulse, the bat is able to compute distance with astonishing precision. In one area of the auditory cortex, we can find neurons which are "tuned" (sensitized) to the delay of emitted and echoed sounds. These neurons respond neither to emitted nor to echoed sound alone, but fire only to pairs of sounds. The remarkable feature of this mechanism is that individual neurons respond to different delays, from a fraction of a millisecond to about 18ms, and that based on this, the animal is able to locate prey at a distance of just under 10cm to 3m.

In investigations of spatial orientation in mice, it was found that various senses participate in the perception of space, including the visual, the auditory and the tactile (for example, the whiskers transmit tactile cues to the appropriate receptors). Accordingly, neuron layers can be found in the brain that map spatial information for each modality, and these neuron layers are situated in relation to each other in such a way as to provide accurate models of the mouse's environment (Drager and Hubel 1975).

Another problem in neurophysiology that has been intensively investigated is the question of how stimuli are transformed into action, and how the animal's brain generates the commands for the motor organs. We give two examples here to illustrate the organization of these mechanisms.

The German ethologist J. P. Ewert (1980) and his team have investigated the prey- and predator-recognizing mechanisms of the European toad (*Bufo bufo*). These toads prey upon smaller animals and are themselves preyed upon by predators that hunt specifically for them, thus presenting them with a considerable perceptual problem. The toad should choose the largest prey-stimulus possible, as within certain size limits catching large prey is the most economical activity, but at the same time it must also be able to recognize the smallest predator that could represent a danger. The toad carefully observes the size of all moving objects passing before it. If the toad is presented in an experiment with some dark squares varying in size, it will react within certain size limits by turning towards them, which is the first action in taking prey. If, however, the squares are above a certain size the toad will stand up tall, displaying one part of its repertoire of escape behaviors.

How can the toad estimate the size of an approaching object? The simplest way would be to calculate the size of the picture projected on to the retina on the basis of the visual angle. The visual angle of an object of a constant size changes with distance, appearing larger close up and smaller further away. At the start of their terrestrial life, toads are unable to establish the distance of objects correctly; instead, they have a preference for objects of a given visual angle. The toads require some weeks of learning in order to be able to estimate the distance of objects correctly.

In addition to the size of a moving object, its shape also provides the toad with important information. If a moving black stripe is shown to the animal against a white background, it reacts in two different ways, depending on the direction of movement of the black stripe. If the stripe moves horizontally, like a worm, the toad immediately turns toward it and tries to catch it. However, if the stripe moves in the direction of the shorter axis, then the toad displays a defensive reaction, puffing itself up. In the first case, the moving stripe was named a *worm*, and in the second case an *anti-worm*.

The neuroanatomical basis of this behavior has been successfully analyzed. The information originating from the image projected onto the retina of the toad is transmitted through the axons of the optic tract to the opposite visual tectum and thalamus. If the neurons of the retina-projection layer of the optic tectum are stimulated electrically, then a freely moving toad will perform an orientation movement in exactly the same direction as it would if the picture of the worm were projected to the proper site of the retinal surface. In contrast, if the retinal projection to the thalamus is stimulated, then the animal produces an avoidance reaction similar to that elicited when a picture of the anti-worm appears.

Two kinds of visual neuron have been found in the tectum. Both types have receptive fields of about 27 degrees and respond to moving objects projected onto the retina. The activity of one type (the t1 cells) does not alter if the stimulus object is enlarged at right angles to the direction of movement (anti-worm), but the firing frequency increases considerably if the object is elongated (worm). The t2 cells increase their activity on the appearance of a worm stimulus, but they decrease it when the anti-worm is presented. In the thalamus, cells have been found (tp1) that have extremely large receptive fields in the retina (46 degrees), and can only be activated by larger objects or by the anti-worm. The different neurons also influence each others' activity. It has been recorded that the firing frequency of the t1 cells increases on presentation of the worm-stimulus, and that this activity stimulates the firing of the t2 cells. On presenting the anti-worm, however, the enhanced activity of the tp1 cells inhibits the firing of the t2 cells. Thus, the t1 and tp1 neurons act as stimulus filters, indicating whether the stimulus is worm-like or anti-worm-like. The interaction between the two kinds of filter neuron strictly separates the neural information eliciting the orientating and defense responses.

Experiments such as these have proved beyond doubt the hypothesis, originating from the behavioral sciences, that one of the most important biological functions of the animal brain is the formation of an internal representation of the external environment in the form of an active dynamic model. The behavior is directed by the neural system, which receives instructions directly from this internal model. Furthermore, the investigation of environmental models in different species has revealed that such models are always species-specific, and that the genetic memory determines from the beginning which aspects of the environment will be built into the neural model constructed by the brain. The environmental model then obtains its final shape from the interaction of the genetic and neural memories.

Genetic Restrictions in the Application of Cognitive Maps

In animals, memory plays an important role in the creation of such cognitive maps of the environment. Cognitive maps, however, are only one of the factors that influence behavior. It is well known that cognitive maps are influenced by behavioral instructions that are determined by the genetic memory.

Observing animals in their natural environment, the American ethologist Alan Kamil has revealed that the cognitive map is of great importance in the life of the nectar-eating honey-bird (Kamil and Balda 1985). The energy requirements of this bird are supplied entirely by sugar derived from floral nectar. Since searching for flowers requires energy, the efficiency of searching is very important; these birds are territorial and defend their flowers. Kamil observed that the honey-bird visits flowers regularly and never returns to the same flower twice in a day. After careful observation, Kamil concluded that a cognitive map that localizes the flowers is formed in the memory of the honey-bird, which makes use of this map during gathering.

Kamil's conclusion is supported by laboratory experiments (Cole et al. 1982), which reveal another very important thing: a cognitive map can be used only for definite purposes and only in a definite way. In the laboratory, honey-birds were presented with a learning task similar to that solved under natural conditions. Colored plastic flowers containing sugar syrup were arranged in a way similar to real flowers in the natural environment. Birds learned easily the features and location of the flowers. Two different tasks were then given to them. In the first experiment, birds were rewarded (with food) only if they chose flowers not visited previously. This task was very similar to the natural one and so the birds were able to learn it easily. After an average of 120 trials they rarely tried to visit the same flower twice. In contrast, the honey-birds in the second experiment were rewarded only when they visited the same flower a second time. The birds had difficulty adapting to this task, and even when they succeeded in learning it, they made many mistakes.

Considering the natural environment, this behavior is quite logical. Nectar production is a slow process. The replenishment of the nectar takes about a day and it is therefore quite pointless to waste energy in visiting flowers that have already been visited on the same day. It is especially interesting that the honey-bird is virtually unable to learn a task that is impractical in its natural environment.

In terms of game theory, the gathering behavior of the honey-bird is referred to as a *win–shift* strategy. The reverse is called a *win–stay* strategy, and these strategies control the behavior of many species. Aside from the shift and stay strategies, several additional rules have been demonstrated to complement the use of cognitive maps.

The most detailed laboratory experiments have been performed using rats. These experiments played a very important part in the discovery of the cognitive map and in the identification of its characteristics. In their experiments, D. S. Olton and co-workers used a radial maze with eight arms made of thin wood. A piece of food was hidden in a hole at the far end of each arm. A hungry rat was placed in the center of the maze and allowed to explore the new environment until it had discovered the covered food at the end of one of the arms. Thereafter, the rat visited the other arms for food. Searching could be performed in several ways: the animal could memorize, for instance, where it had already been and subsequently check only the arms not visited before. Another solution would be to follow a simple rule, such as "go clockwise and check the places one after another." It very quickly became clear, however, that the rat memorizes features of the environment outside the maze, and bases its orientation on these spatial landmarks. When the maze is rotated, the animal continues searching according to the original position.

Using a more complex maze with seventeen arms (built from linen tubes), it has been shown that, although the cognitive map plays the most important role in finding the food, the rat also uses additional behavioral instructions (Olton and Samuelson 1976). The role of memory was demonstrated by an experiment in which rats were forced to wait before entering an arm; in this situation the next choice was random relative to the previous visit. However, efficiency did not decrease and only one or two mistakes were recorded during the course of visiting all seventeen arms. The special behavioral instructions were revealed when the delays were omitted. Under these conditions, rats often moved in a single direction, visiting the arms in a clockwise sequence, for instance. However, this rule seems not to be rigid; rather, it says, "go clockwise (or anticlockwise) into one of the next three or four arms." As we mentioned above, these additional instructions are not seen if a delay of several minutes interrupts searching. In this case, the animal's choice depends exclusively on its memory. It is not simple for a rat to solve the task without the help of the behavioral instructions. However, the animals are able to perform the task successfully using memory traces alone.

In lower animals behavioral instructions play the leading role, since memory is less developed. In experiments with the Siamese fighting fish (*Betta splendens*), a maze-like aquarium was built, with a reward of a tubifex worm placed at the end of each arm. The fish was able to learn to gather the worms, but only when entry to the arms was not delayed. In this case the performance of the animal was, on average, about seven correct choices out of eight opportunities. The fish applied a very effective behavioral instruction. After leaving an arm it always swam into the neighboring compartment. When the search was stopped for only half a minute, the fish was able to remember where the search had been interrupted, and its performance did not decline. However, after a delay of five minutes, the fish forgot everything, and it continued the search randomly, making numerous mistakes. Thus, it can be concluded that the Siamese fighting fish was not able to form a long-lasting cognitive map of the eight-armed aquarium, and that searching was guided only by the behavioral instruction ("go to the neighboring arm") and by the memory trace of the arm last visited (Roitblat, Tham, and Golub 1982).

It has been noted that rats, too, apply the win–shift rule. In one experiment, an eight-armed maze was used. Following the first four choices, the search was stopped for a while. Two experimental groups were formed. The first group was rewarded in the previously unvisited arms, while the animals of the second group could find food only in the arms visited before. The learning performance of the two groups showed a striking difference. The members of the first group acquired the task quickly; approximately thirty trials were sufficient to produce 3.5 right choices on average. In contrast, the second group was unable to learn the task. Their performance only slightly exceeded the success of random choices (as expected without learning), even after fifty trials. It can be concluded that rats use the win–shift strategy (required for solving the first problem) and are unable to learn the win–stay strategy.

The experiment was repeated under more natural conditions. A large chamber was furnished with smaller chambers of various sizes, with tubes (excellent hiding-places), and also with three small towers in which food was hidden. The towers were continuously observed. In the first experiment, all three towers contained food and the rats were seen to visit all the towers and eat some food from each, even though there was plenty of the same food in each of them. The rats did not stop searching for food after consuming food in the first tower. Their behavior was even more unusual when only one of the towers contained food. Rats that chose an empty tower first continued to search as normal, and that tower was not visited again on the same day. The behavior of rats visiting the food-containing tower first was quite similar; the animals consumed some food, after which they left the food-containing tower and visited the other ones. They did not eat for the rest of the day, and failed to return to the tower already visited.

Barnett and Cowan (1976) studied the behavior of rats reared in the central compartment of a cross-shaped maze. The rats were allowed to investigate the rest of the maze for one hour daily. In this experiment, it was also observed that the animals never returned on the same day to the arms already explored. Thus, field exploration in rats is organized according to the win–shift strategy.

The rigidity of the animal mind is striking. The rat can form correct cognitive maps of its environment and has excellent learning abilities, as demonstrated in the seventeen-armed maze. The animal, however, is able to use these precise cognitive maps only in accordance with the genetically coded behavioral strategies. The win–shift strategy is obviously "logical" for rats. When they are searching for food they have to examine their cognitive map for places not visited before. The reverse strategy is illogical for rats; the idea of returning to where they were before simply does not enter their mind. It is likely that the food-searching strategy of the rat is a result of evolution. Rats show no food preferences, and the win–shift strategy ensures the consumption of a large variety of food—although at first sight it exposes them to the danger of eating toxic food. As we will show later, rats learn easily to avoid toxic baits. This type of learning is effective only if the animal consumes small quantities of any kind of new food or of the food found at a new place. The win–shift strategy fulfills these requirements.

The meaning of such behavioral strategies can be understood only in the natural environment of the animal. In honey-birds, only the win–shift strategy ensures the required amount of energy; while the win–stay food-searching strategy is appropriate for ovenbirds, since maggots are always located in patches. These strategies reflect certain characteristics of the natural environment. They are elements of an environmental model formed in the brain and represent definite and specific relations between the components of the environment. Using "ready-made" model-elements, the animal is able to create a model that describes its environment exactly. It is obvious that if the animal is removed from its environment or the environment is changed in some way, the behavior of the animal may become completely inappropriate and meaningless.

Animal Cultures

Recent investigations have suggested that the transmission of experience may be an important factor for survival in animals that live in groups. The main features of the transmission of experience are as follows:

(1) a given behavior spreads within the group by learning;
(2) the transfer of experience also occurs between generations; and
(3) remote or separated populations show different forms of the given behavior.

Since these are similar to the most important features of human culture, the term *animal culture* has recently been accepted for various forms of transmitted experience within animal groups: the imitation of movement patterns, transmission of foraging techniques, transmission of song dialects from one generation to the next, recognition of special kinds of food by learning, and other similar behavioral forms (Mundinger 1980). In the following pages we describe several examples of animal culture in which imitation (copying) plays the leading role in the spread of experience.

A resident of the seashore, the oystercatcher (*Haematopus ostralegus*) forages mostly on mussels and refines its foraging technique by intensive learning. At first, parents feed their young in the nest, then in the close vicinity of the nest, and finally on the seashore. The birds use two different techniques to open the shells—both of them are the result of repeated attempts and intensive learning. Birds using the "hammer-stroke" technique place the mussel on firm ground, knock a hole with their bill in the thinnest part of the shell, and then pull out the edible parts through the hole. The other technique is called "stabbing." In this case, birds attack the shellfish under the water, when the water-perfusing siphon of their prey is just visible. The birds stab their bills suddenly into the opening and cut the hinge of the shells with a skillful movement.

A given bird uses only one of the two available techniques. For a long time it was believed that oystercatchers form two different sub-species, with the two techniques resulting from genetic differences. It was the English ethologist Norton-Griffiths (1969) who demonstrated, by clever experiments, that youngsters learn the technique from their parents. When chicks were exchanged between parents using different techniques, the young always acquired the technique used by their foster parents.

Just as oystercatchers learn the difficult shell-opening technique, so several species of passerine birds learn their songs from their parents. In the course of "mobbing," birds also learn which species to regard as predators by imitating conspecifics. It can be predicted exactly what, when, and how a given animal will learn from conspecifics.

In this section, we shall deal with learning forms that are occasional rather than predictable. These demonstrate that higher animals, at least, are able to acquire special behavioral patterns purely by observing the behavior of conspecific animals. Learning of this type occurs mainly when it results in a well-defined benefit.

An illustrative example is seen in the behavior of a group of African elephants, as documented by Curio, Ernst, and Vieth (1978). In 1919, orange groves were established on an area that was often rifled by a resident population of more than a hundred elephants. The farmers hired an elephant hunter to kill off the animals. The hunter killed the animals one by one, so that their death and suffering were observed by their companions. One year later only twenty to twenty-five elephants were still living. The farmers made a concerted attempt to get rid of the remaining population, but the task of the hunter became more and more difficult because the elephants learned to be extremely cautious. They noticed the smallest movement from a great distance, and they switched to nocturnal activity. After numerous attempts, the hunter and the farmers had to acknowledge that they were not able to exterminate the elephants completely. They founded the Addo park, a closed bushy area of 10,000 hectares in the hills, which represented a suitable shelter for the surviving elephants. More than sixty years have passed since that time, and presumably none of the animals surviving the original massacre is now living. Despite this fact, this elephant population is the most dangerous one in the whole of Africa. They have continued to live nocturnally, and they still respond with extreme aggression to humans even though nobody has assaulted them since the foundation of the park.

In the laboratory it is easy to carry out experiments demonstrating the ability of animals to learn from one another. There are popular legends about the bait-recognition ability of rats, which were discussed in detail above. This knowledge is thought to be transmitted from one generation of rats to the next. B. G. Galef, the Canadian ethologist, decided to check the validity of this legend by laboratory experiments. Using Norwegian rats, he asked whether poison-avoidance would appear in the offspring of a mother conditioned previously by poisoned food. A large room was divided into several compartments, each equipped with television cameras to observe the rats. In the course of the experiments, the legend was shown to be true. Young rats avoided the food that was avoided by the parents, particularly the mother. Imitation was demonstrated to be based on three factors. Young rats initially prefer the feeding grounds of their parents, and in this way they consume almost exclusively the food consumed by their parents. Later, when they forage alone, they still show a preference for these familiar foods. The second factor is the mother's milk. By clever experiments, Galef succeeded in demonstrating that preferences related to various food flavors are literally "sucked in with the milk," since young prefer the foods consumed by their mother during the suckling period. The flavoring compounds penetrate into the milk, and later guide the taste preferences of the young. The third factor had already been observed by previous investigators of poison-avoidance. Rats often urinate on unpalatable foods (or on foods that, through conditioning, they have learned to be unpalatable), and these foods are avoided even by in-experienced animals. Together, these experiments clearly demonstrate that rats are able to transmit food-preferences to future generations by social learning. However, considering the phenomenon as a whole, food-avoidance is clearly based on the contribution of several inherited behaviors. The role of learning is only to ensure the remembrance of places and flavors. The animals do not learn food-avoidance itself by observing the behavior of other animals, and in this type of social learning genetic memory plays the leading role (Galef 1976).

Two Italian researchers, Gandolfi and Parisi, noticed that among rat populations living along the Po river, there are some animals that obtain their food in a quite special way (see Olton and Samuelson 1976). They dive into the river for clams, which they then open and eat on the bank. At the same time, Gandolfi and Parisi also observed sympatric populations in which this habit was completely unknown. According to the Italian researchers, this represents an unusually clear case of observational learning. It is highly probable that the rats learn this new way of foraging from each other. The knowledge survives within a relatively restricted colony, and its spread into other colonies is very slow. It would be almost impossible to demonstrate the validity of this theory by field observations, which persuaded Galef to perform appropriate laboratory experiments.

The experimental apparatus consisted of a home cage connected to a small swimming pool by a tunnel. Food and water were provided ad libitum in the home cage and the rats were also allowed to visit the swimming pool freely through the tunnel. The behavior of the animals was continuously recorded on videotape. The first question Galef asked was whether adult animals are able to learn underwater foraging from each other. Instead of clams, he used chocolate, a favorite food of rats. A particular animal was trained to dive into the 15cm-deep water for chocolate pieces previously placed there. The chocolate pieces were not covered by water at first; then they were covered by a thin layer of water, the depth of which was increased by 1–2cm each day. After the rat had learned to gather the chocolate pieces quickly and skillfully, untrained animals (adult siblings of the same age) were placed in the cage. The experiment lasted several weeks. Galef wanted to find out whether the inexperienced animals would imitate this technique of chocolate-gathering. None of the twenty naive animals used in the experiment was able to imitate the trained one, despite the fact that they often followed the trained individual into the swimming pool, observed his behavior, and even tried to steal the just-collected chocolate.

In a further experiment, Galef trained several female rats to gather the chocolate hidden under the water. When the females were able to perform the task, their 3-week-old offspring were placed in the cage for several weeks. Four out of eighteen young animals succeeded in imitating the behavior of their mother, and acquired the technique of chocolate-gathering. This experiment demonstrated clearly that rats are in fact able to learn new foraging techniques, although only during their youth. Later it was revealed that some young rats are able to acquire the new technique by themselves, especially those previously used to swimming. Animals able to swim showed much greater willingness to search spontaneously under water. These experiments confirmed the Italian researchers' hypothesis regarding the appearance and spread of clam-foraging rat populations in nature.

Similar experiments have been performed by psychologists using the popular Skinner box (e.g. Schwartz 1984). The box used in these experiments was divided into two equal parts by a transparent wall. A small lever was placed symmetrically on each side of the partition, and a group of animals was trained to obtain water by pressing the lever. After a short period of water deprivation, the trained rats were placed individually in one side the box, and naive animals in the other. The trained rats immediately began to press the lever to obtain water, and drank the small portions of water greedily. Observing this, sooner or later the naive animals began to show similar behavior and learned how to obtain water much faster than control animals, which were allowed to operate the lever but had no neighbor or only an inexperienced partner on the other side of the wall. This experiment clearly supports the idea that the rat brain is somehow able to transform visual information about the behavior of another animal into its own behavioral instructions.

Since this time, similar experiments have been performed in birds. By watching trained animals, dwarf quail (*Excalfactoria chinensis*) are quickly able to learn to peck an illuminated spot to obtain food. The Hungarian ethologist L. Sasvári (1979) performed similar experiments with tits. He revealed that tits easily learn from trained animals to obtain food hidden in a cloth-covered hole by drawing the cloth aside. An extremely interesting observation made by Sasvári was that tits show a willingness to learn mainly from conspecifics. If one great tit (*Parus major*) observes the new foraging technique in another great tit, it is highly probable that it will acquire the technique. If the tutor animal is a blue tit (*Parus caeruleus*), then the probability of imitation is reduced. Young animals tend to imitate more easily the example of another species.

Japanese ethologists have established a group of Japanese macaques (*Macaca fuscata*) on a small sea island and observed them over a long period. One of their findings has become world famous: they reported that a juvenile female, named Imo, "discovered" a new foraging technique. The researchers fed the animals regularly on seeds strewn over the bare ground. The macaques liked this kind of food very much, and therefore picked the seeds from out of the dust one by one. Imo discovered that if she took sand and seeds to the beach and threw them into the water, the sand and the dust would sink down, and the clean seeds remain on the surface, to be gathered easily. However, the most interesting phenomenon occurred later. Imo was very young when she discovered the technique, and therefore, as the observations confirmed, none of the group members living at that time imitated her. Had the monkeys lost their famous imitative ability? Several years later the new, young members of the group (lower ranking than Imo in the social hierarchy) began to imitate her, and in the next ten to fifteen years the habit became widespread in the group (Kawai 1965).

Thus even the fate of such a "discovery" is under genetic control. The acquisition of useful skills may be started by particular individuals and in definite ways, even in monkeys. In fact, only in the last few years has the interest of ethologists turned toward the mechanism of imitative learning. In the 1950s, English ethologists had already reported that in England tits "discovered" how to open milk bottles covered by aluminum foil (Hinde and Fischer 1952). By this means, they could steal the cream floating at the top of the bottles, which were brought to the houses each morning and placed on the doorsteps. The habit presumably spread by observational learning. When it was first noticed, the behavior was characteristic of only a small area; later it spread out concentrically among the tits at a speed of approximately 30km per year. All this was reported thirty years ago, and only recently have proper laboratory investigations of the phenomenon been performed, by two Canadian ethologists, Palametta and Lefebvre (Schwartz 1984). They investigated the existence of similar observational-learning mechanisms in pigeons.

The task was very similar to that performed by the tits. Seeds were hidden in a small box, and the box covered with a sheet of thin paper. At first, inexperienced pigeons did not know what to do with the box placed in their cage, and probably could not even suppose that it contained food. However, the pigeons could be trained to peck a hole in the paper to reach the seeds. As a first step, the experimenters cut a small hole in the paper covering the box, and put a seed into it. The pigeons discovered the seed and began to enlarge the hole to obtain additional seeds. Later they were able to make a hole by themselves. The experiment described below was performed using similarly trained pigeons.

Twenty naive pigeons were divided into four groups and were placed individually into the left side of a large cage divided in two by a transparent plastic wall. In a control group, naive animals had no visual contact with the trained ones, and none of them opened a seed-filled covered box placed in the cage. In the three remaining groups, a trained "tutor" pigeon was placed in the opposite side of the cage. However, only one trained group was provided with the same seed-filled, covered box. As they had learned, the tutors in this group opened the box and consumed the seeds, and all the naive pigeons able to observe their behavior quickly learned to open their own box. In the third group, the tutor animals were provided with an already opened box, and thus began to eat immediately, without first pecking a hole. Their naive counterparts also learned to open the box, although they required more time for this learning than the previous group. Finally, the tutor pigeons of the fourth group were provided with covered but empty boxes. Of course they could not know this in advance, and consequently opened the box. As a result, their naive counterparts could observe only the opening phase, without information concerning the purpose of the action, and the naive pigeons of this group did not acquire the task.

The experiment leaves no doubt that pigeons are able to learn a complex food-obtaining technique by observation only. However, this occurs only when all phases, including food-consumption, are presented. Let us consider what a complex task must be performed here by the pigeon's brain. It demonstrates that a pigeon is able to include into its environmental model neutral stimuli like the box, the hole-preparing movements, and the image of the feeding conspecific, in such a way as to place itself in the position of another animal performing the observed actions. These facts lead inevitably to the conclusion that pigeons must possess the ability to think.

In the preceding pages we have seen that the ability to transmit learned behavior from generation to generation, and so to influence the behavior of whole groups or societies, is not unique to human experience. Human beings, however, have elevated this ability to a unique level with unprecedented consequences for human cultures, as we will see in Chapter 2, on the cognitive maps of societies.

Cognitive Maps in Children

We can now move back to humans and briefly examine the development of cognitive maps during childhood.

Perhaps the earliest maps that infants acquire are behavioral. In plain English, this means that very early in their lives infants acquire the ability to imitate simple motor activities that they have seen their parents, for example, perform. The details of the development of these early maps have been studied by the psychologists Mandler (1988) and Bandura (1989). The latter emphasized the importance of the child's attention. What catches the attention is what is retained in the memory and later reenacted through imitation. This form of learning—imitation learning, or learning to behave like a parent or other model—is coming to be recognized as a central feature of infant and childhood learning, and may well play an underestimated role in adult behavior.

Perhaps no one has investigated the development of the overall spectrum of cognitive abilities in children as thoroughly as the Swiss psychologist Jean Piaget. Piaget (Piaget and Inhelder 1971) and the American psychologist Jerome Bruner (Bruner, Olver, and Greenfield 1966) have described the growth of mental representations in children in terms so similar that we will describe them both together as a single account. According to this account, the first year of life is marked by the early appearance of *sensory–motor* depictions of actions, or in other words behavioral reenactments exactly as described in the paragraph above.

According to Piaget and Bruner, the second year of life is marked by the appearance of static, *iconic*, images or maps that the child has little ability to manipulate. Such images center rigidly on the child's own perspective, whether it be of the physical or of the social environment. A child can be asked, for example, to describe a table-top landscape that includes several farm animals, a small lake, and a papier-mâché mountain, all as seen from the eyes of a doll placed nearby on the table. He will do a passable job of this, if he is near the doll and his own perspective is also that of the doll. When asked to walk to the other side of the table, however, and again to describe the landscape as seen by the doll, which has not been moved, his description changes dramatically to his own physical perspective, and utterly disregards the view from the side of the table where the doll remains, and where he was in fact just standing. The child is said to be *perceptually bound.* Switching momentarily to the level of social maps, is it any wonder that such a child may also appear to be self-centered, inflexible, and without true empathy, though he may, in fact, be kind and even compassionate?

By about seven years of age, the child develops the beginnings of a system of flexible symbol manipulations based on a growing language facility. As this system interacts with the internal imagery of the child, a compliant mapping facility develops, able to be manipulated and projected as anticipations of future situations. In this agility we see the beginnings of the full adult potential to create cognitive maps.

Along these lines, Harvard psychologist Stephen Kosslyn (1980), the foremost researcher on visual imagery, observes a notable increase in the ability of adults, over children, to access specific information swiftly and efficiently from internal representations. Thus, an adult, for example, can quickly zoom in on a particular region of a memorized road map, or page of written notes, to gain the desired details.

Cultural Maps

Starting from earliest infancy and continuing throughout life, human cognitive maps accumulate an increasingly rich array of representations that, taken as a whole, portray a person's entire cultural experience. The cultural landscape encoded in such maps includes not only society's conventional patterns of behavior, but its moral values, aesthetic preferences, and spiritual aspirations. In adults, this wondrously complex panorama is divided into overlapping sectors that chart individual life domains such as professional activities, family roles, and religious commitments.

In the 1950s, social theorist Kenneth Boulding (1956) suggested the thoroughly postmodern notion that people project images of cultural reality that then become reality itself, a point we have already touched on earlier in this book. Such an idea is suggestive of a cybernetic circuit, or positive-feedback loop, in which maps of reality are projected out from the person, who then meets up with them in the physical and social environment, and in so doing is forced to affirm or reject their authenticity. This process of authentication, however, depends on the situational context, as well as on the existing maps and the flexibility and creativity of the individual. A piece of driftwood is not a work of art until someone brings it into the house and puts it on the coffee table. Only then does it begin to disclose its aesthetic subtleties. The treatment of women as an underclass is not a moral problem until someone "recognizes" it as such, and then it begins to present itself in increasing clarity.

Like the two apparent sides of a Möbius strip, realities and the maps that project them are one and the same thing. This is a rolling process in which map and reality are transformed into each other. We discover in this image the *process* aspect of both reality and cognitive maps. Both are subject to constant change as they are updated, either by new experiences with the world outside the individual, or by shifts in perspective brought about by ongoing changes within the person.

With these ideas in mind, we might well expect to find that within a single culture, different individuals would have significantly different cognitive maps, depending on their own unique experiences and personalities. We know this to be true from our own personal experience. Moreover, in the large societies of today's world, there are many subcultures with their own attitudes, value systems, and so on. Studies have shown, for example, that within the subcultures of a single city, people from different social and economic groups draw surprisingly different physical maps of the city (Lynch 1960).

In an informal demonstration of the individual variability of cognitive maps, an associate of one of our colleagues asked undergraduate college students to draw maps of the university campus. Those who commuted to the university tended to include sizable parking lots on their maps, while those who lived on campus often omitted the parking lots entirely. Interestingly, the maps seemed to differ according to the student's field of study. Literature and philosophy students drew a large library building near the center of the campus, while business and accounting students displayed a disturbing tendency to include no library at all! Physics and math students sketched in a sizable computer center, while students of literature were likely to leave it out. The building where each student spent most of his or her time was likely to be represented near the center of the campus, while other buildings often got pushed out to the edges. But let us return to the matter of cognitive maps and culture.

Human cultures are represented in many physical objects. These range from works of art, to books, clothing, cities, and instruments of technology. A living culture, however, must also survive in the minds of the people who comprise it. In other words, the knowledge and cultural heritage that is encoded in physical objects such as art, books, and technology, does not comprise a living culture without the active participation of the subjective knowledge that is available only to the mind.

It is useful to consider a human culture as a flowing evolutionary system that involves both physical cultural objects and the ever-changing cognitive maps of individuals (Laszlo 1987a; Artigiani 1988). This whole fluid structure can be seen as an organic configuration that changes over time, thriving or dying out like other evolutionary processes. As we will emphasize below, a growing and vigorous culture undergoes constant transformation, adjusting to changes such as technological developments, influences from other cultures, and events in the natural environment. One thinks, for example, of the classical Greek culture at the time of Pericles, or of the European Renaissance. Cultures that fail to make such adjustments become static and rigid, and are likely to die out if confronted by major challenges.

If we look at a culture as an evolving system, one formed on one side by the physical objects of the culture, and on the other by the cognitive maps of its members, we begin to see how it recreates itself from day to day, year to year, and generation to generation. Cultural objects such as books and works of art play an obvious and important role in transmitting culture, but on their own they are static and inert. The life of a culture is communicated directly by its members, their stories, their myths, their dances, their crafts and skills, passed directly from individual to individual. The entire cycle is animated and carried forward in the projected realities, or maps, of the people who comprise the culture. This process of continuous recreation places human cultures in a broad category of complex and flexible systems, the hallmark of which is their ability and passion for self-creation.

Human cultures, like the eddies of the mountain stream, are cyclic patterns that never quite repeat themselves. The overall form of the culture is always in a state of dynamic change or evolution. Such change may be relatively rapid, as is the case in the art world of New York City, or it may be slow, as was the case with ancient Egypt, which changed amazingly little over the entire millennia. Viewed from a particular moment in history, however, each culture represents a unique dynamic pattern, a particular configuration that usually remains relatively stable from year to year, decade to decade, and sometimes from century to century.

Each culture has its own unique qualities, which it transmits forward as it creates itself into the future. Some cultures, like the Europe of the Middle Ages, are strongly religious, while others are dominantly secular. Some, like classical Greece, place a high value on artistic expression, while many others do not. Some, like historical China, place significant value on tradition, while many modern cultures lack this emphasis. Some value democracy, while others prefer monarchy.

Given such obvious variation in style between different cultures, and realizing that these represent particular attractors, leads naturally to the question of whether certain general types of cultures can be distinguished within the remarkable diversity of past and present societies. So far, at least two notable efforts have been made to model a wide range of cultures in terms of dynamic systems. One of these efforts is by pioneering systems mathematician Ralph Abraham (1989, 1992), and the other is by the social theorist Riane Eisler (1987). Abraham's work is predicated, in turn, on certain thoughts of the prominent anthropologist Ruth Benedict (Maslow and Honigmann

1970), which date back to as long ago as the early 1940s. This story is worth telling.

It seems that Ruth Benedict was haunted by the realization that certain cultures were simply "nicer" to live in than others. Life in these nicer cultures seemed to be pleasant if not downright joyful. People worked together for the good of all, and few if any individuals were permanently rejected or condemned by others. These societies typically believed in benevolent cosmologies, ones in which, for instance, gods and goddesses looked favorably upon human beings.

The cultures that were not nice to live in were those in which individuals strove for power and status at the expense of others, and in which people could be humiliated or entirely rejected by the community. Typically, such cultures lived under oppressive cosmologies in which, for instance, angry, cruel, or indifferent gods required endless appeasement.

Searching for a theme that could clarify the essential difference between these two types of cultures, Benedict came up with the concept of *synergy*. She explained it in her 1941 Bryn Mawr lectures, in which she stated:

I shall need a term for this gamut, a gamut that runs from one pole, where any act or skill that advantages the individual at the same time advantages the group, to the other pole, where every act that advantages the individual is at the expense of others. I shall call this gamut *synergy* . . . I shall speak of cultures with low synergy, where the social structure provides for acts that are mutually opposed and counteractive, and of cultures with high synergy, where it provides for acts that are mutually reinforcing. (Maslow and Honigmann 1970: 324)

In the early 1940s, however, such thoughts were tantamount to heresy. Anthropology, much by dent of Benedict's own efforts, had recently discredited the whole business of ethnocentrism. To suggest that some cultures were in any way superior to others would have been to open a Pandora's box of criticism and misinterpretation. Perhaps for these reasons, or perhaps because of her ensuing involvement in the war effort, Dr Benedict chose not to publish the sizable manuscript on which she had based her lectures. Instead, she gave it for safe-keeping to a friend, Abraham Maslow. He was later to become the leading force in humanistic psychology, but in those days he was still a graduate student. A few years later he suffered a heart attack, and grew concerned that he was not a safe custodian for it. He returned it to Benedict, but when she died in 1948, it was nowhere to be found and, indeed, has not been found since. Fortunately, one of Maslow's own graduate students, John J. Honigmann, had the opportunity to read it while it was in Maslow's possession. Recognizing its importance, he copied sizable portions of it on a manual typewriter. These were to be its only record. Later, he himself became a prominent anthropologist, and in 1970, with Maslow, published these portions of Benedict's manuscript in *American Anthropologist,* from which the above quote is taken.

Maslow had been fascinated by the humanistic implications of the synergy concept, and wrote of it in *Eupsychian Management,* published in 1965. At that time it received considerable discussion in management circles, but it has since fallen into obscurity. Ralph Abraham's (1989, 1992) recent mathematical treatment of synergy brings new vitality to it by exploring its meaning as a cultural attractor. Abraham approaches synergy from the point of view of dynamic systems theory. His work is mathematically sophisticated and will not be treated in detail here, but it is hoped that, when actualized as computer simulations, it will provide a powerful method of social analysis.

It is a general characteristic of highly complex systems, whether they be businesses, individual organisms, or ecologies, that they exhibit certain sensitive pivot points at which a small pressure applied in judicious fashion can dramatically influence the future evolution of the system. It is Abraham's hope that sufficiently large and complex simulations of human societies, and ultimately the world culture, will disclose the sensitive points at which the action of even a few people, applied judiciously, can influence this culture toward a better world.

Riane Eisler's (1987, 1995) work, like that of Ruth Benedict, is also based on a broad review of human societies. While Benedict considered a wide geographic range of societies that still existed during the first half of the twentieth century, Eisler developed her ideas from a penetrating analysis of history. This history goes all the way back to the ancient Magdalenian culture that produced the cave paintings of southern Europe.

The basic idea in Eisler's thought is that the major human cultures have tended to fall into two distinguishable configurations, which are centrally defined by differing gender orientations. She terms these configurations the *dominator* and the *gylanic* ethics. The dominator ethic is already familiar to us. It is characterized by the rule of a small, elite class of individuals, almost always male, who control the major assets of the culture. These individuals tend to dominate the other members of the society in hierarchically ordered regimes, with women forming an underclass that has little control over its own fate. In such societies, weapons represent the leading technologies, and war is a principal means of the acquisition of wealth. Dominator societies value the obedi-ence of their members, who find safety only in conformity. Leaders are threatened by the appearance of creativity, individualism, and deep inquiries after truth. They rule by dint of fear. Women are often the object of the unsolicited aggression of males, and the men are largely unaccountable for acts of brutality against women.

Gylanic cultures are fundamentally egalitarian. The term *gylany* is taken from the Greek word *gyne*, or woman, here connected to *an*, from *andros*, the Greek word for man (Eisler 1987). The defining character-istic of gylanic cultures is a balanced relationship between men and women. Relationships in general are characterized by partnership and lateral linkage rather than by dominance and hierarchy. Value is placed on individual creativity, education, and the pursuit of truth. Technology is directed toward the mutual benefit of the members of the society, and war plays no role whatsoever unless it is inflicted from without.

Eisler's basic notion is that these two types of societies represent major attractors into which cultural systems can be drawn. The descrip-tion of dominator culture above seems all too familiar in Western history and, unfortunately, is easily recognized in the world today. We might even ask if there are any significant examples of gylanic societies beyond exotic instances such as a few South Sea Island cultures. Can we, in fact, find an instance of a major civilization that actually flourished under the gylanic regime? It turns out that archeological research seems to have unearthed just such a civilization, one that to a striking extent fits the gylanic ideal.

In recent decades a significant re-evaluation of archeological findings from the neolithic age in Eastern Europe and the Middle East has brought to light an entire civilization that flourished prior to the rise of ancient Egypt and Mesopotamia. The ascendance of this civilization, which archeologist Marija Gimbutas (1982) calls *Old Europe*, lasted for three thousand years, from roughly 6500 to 3500BCE. Agriculture provided its principal source of material wealth. At its peak, Old Europe produced religious art (pottery and frescoes), fine clothing, and evidently had the time and energy for joyful celebration. The cosmol-ogy of this culture centered around images of the Earth Goddess. A vast number of small statuettes from this period represent the goddess with exaggerated breasts and hips, in some instances in the act of childbirth, all suggestive of the nurturing, fertile, feminine aspect of the earth.

This civilization seems to have been remarkably egalitarian. Though the feminine values of nurturance, mutual support, and creativity were central, it was not a matriarchal society in the usual sense. In round burial sites, for instance, women are found at the center, with men near the edge, suggesting that women were of higher status than men. Both sexes, however, were well dressed and in possession of ornaments and personal items that suggest that both were recipients of honor and respect. This contrasts dramatically with later burials in Greece and elsewhere, where the position of honor was held by a single warlord who was buried with his spears and shields.

Old Europe seems to have been peaceful beyond anything experienced since. Clean and comfortable cities and villages were positioned for beauty and convenience rather than for defense. There are virtually no weapons among the artifacts of this civilization, and the motifs of its art were of nature and the goddess rather than battles.

The point of all of this is that, if the evidence of three thousand and more years is to be believed, the gylanic way of life seems to be a major cultural attractor. Unfortunately, this attractor was gradually destabilized by the influx of increasing numbers of warlike nomadic tribes, who either conquered the Old Europeans or simply moved in on them, degrading their value system to that of their own. Many of these nomads originated on the steppes of Russia. Their migration has been traced by the southern and western spread of the barrow graves in which they buried their dead. Gimbutas (1982) called these invaders *kurgans*, after the Russian word *kurgan*, or barrow.

The demise of Old Europe was followed by a dark age that lasted until the rise of the "ancient world" of Egypt, Mesopotamia, and Greece during the last two to three millennia before Christ. The value system— indeed, the entire attractor for those new societies—however, was more kurgan than Old European. This was especially true of Mesopotamia and Greece. The warrior–king had replaced what had probably been a queen in the old culture. Warlike sky deities such as Zeus, Marduk, and Yahweh replaced the earth goddess. Hierarchies replaced equality, with male warriors and priests at the top and woman far down the line. Glory was to be achieved in battle, and aggression became institutionalized as noble and heroic. The entire dominator attractor had arisen in full ascendance.

This is not to say that there was nothing of deep value in the new civilizations or in their religions. They were the great cultural forebears of our own civilization. They gave us writing, art and architecture, and the great religious motifs that still remain with us today. The masculine visage of the transcendent carries a majesty, wisdom, and authority that is different from that of the feminine, though it can also be terrible in its destructive potency. The bottom line, however, is that the dominator ethic, even at its best, amounts to good living for only a select few, and through its inherent tendency toward aggression, and its repression of individual freedom and creativity, inflicts a great cost on its members in terms of the loss of the life fully lived. And, in the world today, its penchant for aggression and war make it a grave danger for the entire human species, together with the whole web of life on Earth.

Moral Maps

Let us turn for the moment to a different topic, one of notable concern to the modern world. This is the matter of moral sensitivity. David Loye wrote:

If we look into the future, as we continually must, one thing above all is apparent. It is that of all the "cognitive maps" our species has evolved over more than a million years of living on this earth, we have at last reached a time where one map above all is of overriding importance. This is our cognitive map of what we call ethics, or moral development. (1990: 41)

By far the most prominent theory of moral development today is that of Harvard psychologist Lawrence Kohlberg (1984). The essential notion in Kohlberg's thought is that moral development follows a developmental progression through a sequence of stages not unlike Jean Piaget's stages of intellectual development. In support of his theory, Kohlberg and his students have conducted a considerable number of extensive interviews with individuals of many nationalities throughout the world. The approach used in these investigations is to present people with moral dilemmas and ask them to reason these through aloud. The maturity of their moral thinking is judged on the basis of the type of reasoning that they use, and not on the solutions themselves. For instance, the investigator might describe a situation in which a man cannot afford to buy medication for a seriously ailing spouse. Should he steal the medication or not, and why? The answer yes or no is not important to Kohlberg, but the reasoning behind it discloses the individual's level of moral attainment.

Kohlberg's theory sees moral development as passing through three major developmental levels. Although there has been more than one version of the theory, its most widely understood form posits three major levels of development, with two stages in each, thus giving a total sequence of six stages. This sequence can be observed in the development of moral maturity in the child (Lickona 1983). Few adults, however, reach the highest levels, and indeed, Kohlberg's principal interest was with the moral judgments of adults, not children.

The three levels in Kohlberg's theory are referred to as *preconventional, conventional,* and *postconventional.* As the terms suggest, they indicate that the development of moral maturity passes from an early, preconventional level, through a conventional level, in which moral judgment is based on conventional social standards, and on to a level beyond the conventional standards of society. Preconventional morality is based simply on avoiding pain (stage one) or obtaining pleasure (stage two). The pop phrase "If it feels good, do it!" is an example of a preconventional moral attitude. It is not really a moral posture at all, but simply a self-serving rule for making decisions. Unfortunately, many adults do not pass beyond this level.

The first stage of conventional morality simply involves going along with the group. This orientation is frequently seen among adolescents. If a student at this stage is caught cheating on a test, he is likely to defend himself by pointing out that others cheat as well. In other words, he defends his behavior as complying with group standards. At the next stage, however, morality takes on absolute standards. These can be given by a parent, by religious dogma, or by the law. The important point is that the individual accepts these standards as absolute. Morality is a black-and-white affair, and there is no bargaining with it.

Kohlberg found that most adult Europeans and Americans, even college-educated ones, make moral judgments at the conventional level. A few, however, make judgments at the highest, postconventional level. Moral reasoning at the first of the two postconventional stages is based on the realization that it is, in fact, people who ultimately select moral standards. Laws, for instance, represent the considered judgment of society about right behavior. With this in mind, the person at this stage is likely to ask whether a particular act is in line with the law, and beyond this, whether it is in the spirit of the law as well. He or she might question a particular law, or church dogma, as contrary to the original intentions of those who formulated it. Thus, a person in this stage might engage in citizenly activities, including civil disobedience, directed at changing an unjust law. Not surprisingly, this stage is sometimes termed the *legalistic* orientation.

The highest stage of postconventional morality—the highest moral orientation in Kohlberg's system—involves what Kohlberg referred to as *individual principles of conscience.* This rare stage is most dramatically seen in persons such as Mahatma Gandhi and Martin Luther King, Jr. Though such individuals may sometimes seem to stand alone against their peers, Kohlberg supposed that they represent abstract universal principles of compassion and concern for all of humanity.

Kohlberg believed that growth occurs when people with different moral orientations interact. When moral issues are discussed openly, the person with the lower standard is at a disadvantage beside one with the higher level of development, who, having once been at the lower level himself, is already familiar with his arguments. The result of such interactions is that the morally advanced individual is unlikely to be moved by the less mature person, while the latter experiences some degree of discomfort. In time, he is likely to find his own moral judgments ascending toward those of the more advanced person.

Interestingly, Kohlberg found that most of the time each individual operates from a single orientation, that is, from one particular stage. He or she has some feeling, however, for the stages immediately above and below. When in the company of others who are at one of these stages he is likely to fall in with them and behave as if he were at their stage, whether it is just above or just below his own. On the other hand, he does not really understand the morality of those who are two or more stages above. For instance, a person in either of the conventional stages of morality is unlikely to understand someone like Mahatma Gandhi as anything beyond an oddity. Such oddities can become quite annoying if, for example, they are petitioning for environmental conservation issues at the cost of preconventional rewards or conventional standards to which the forest, lake, or species has been subject.

Now, let us consider Kohlberg's overall system in terms of cognitive maps. Doing so presents us with a different kind of moral hierarchy. Preconventional morality, with its emphasis on rewards and punishments, seems to be governed by cognitive maps of the most concrete variety. These are of the sort studied by Tolman (1932) in rats, which represent the lay of the environment between me and the object of my pleasure or pain. There seems no reason to think that more abstract agendas are involved.

Conventional morality involves more abstract cultural maps. At the absolute morality stage, for instance, one must interpret the mandates of authority in terms of the particular situation in which one finds oneself. The results are neither flexible nor creative, but represent the use of the maps of cultural norms taken as absolute dictates of moral conduct. The first postconventional or legalistic orientation also draws on such maps, but seems to make use of them in a more flexible manner. Here, individuals seem to have acquired a certain ability to put distance between themselves and the map. They are able to make some assessment of the general lay of the land, noting details that seem inconsistent with the whole—violations of the spirit of the law. In making such assessments, the postconventional person achieves the important recognition that cultural maps are human constructions. Thus, such a person can assume the prerogative to change them.

Individuals with the legalistic orientation are reflective, but are not necessarily self-reflective. They view the cultural map with an air of objectivity not possible for one who is entirely conventionally oriented. When such persons become self-reflective, however, they must consider their own relationship to the cultural map, a relationship that in time must come to include their own deepest personal feelings. If they continue to explore this relationship, they may begin to articulate a very personal value map that may or may not conform to cultural norms. If it does not, they must choose between their own standards and those of the collective. In this dialectic between self-reflective personal values and those of the culture at large, we find the genesis of Kohlberg's highest stage of moral development. In it, we have moved to a self-reflective consciousness that characterizes the very essence of the self. We might say that moral judgment at this stage arises directly from the recursive self, rather than from ordinary cultural maps.

One critic of Kohlberg's theory, psychologist Carol Gilligan (1982), argues that his entire approach to morality basically concerns *individuals* and how they resolve their differences, terming it a *morality of justice*, and contrasts it with an alternative system that she calls a *morality of care*. She suggests that the morality of justice is largely a male point of view, while concerns such as caring and compassion are more typically valued by women. She points out that much of Kohlberg's research was conducted with boys or men. In fact, his doctoral study was done solely with boys. Gilligan, on the other hand, interviewed a number of pregnant women about an eminent moral dilemma: their personal confrontation with the issue of abortion. She found only three distinct levels of moral growth, and these differed from those of Kohlberg.

The first of Gilligan's levels is characterized as *self-interest*. Here, the decision of whether or not to have an abortion is made on the basis of personal gain or loss. I will have an abortion, for instance, because a baby would be a burden to my life-style. The second level of moral development was that of *self-sacrifice*. For example, I will have the baby for my husband. The third and final level, *nonviolence*, represents a shift to a balanced regard for the well-being of everyone concerned, including oneself. For instance, one woman stated that going ahead with the pregnancy would not be a favor to either herself or the baby.

Viewing Gilligan's theory in terms of cognitive maps, we find that it has some features in common with Kohlberg's system. In particular, her lowest level of moral development, self-interest, is much like his preconventional level, and likewise would seem to utilize the most concrete variety of cognitive maps. Her self-sacrifice level seems at first sight to be different from Kohlberg's conventional morality. Given, however, that self-sacrifice has been a traditional role for women, it is not clear that this is not really another type of conventional behavior. The principal difference between the two systems would seem to lie at the very highest levels, namely Kohlberg's principles of conscience and Gilligan's level of nonviolence. Viewing them in terms of cognitive maps, however, suggests that even these have an essential feature in common. This is that both seem to arise from the self-reflective stance that brings one into relationship with both the cultural value maps and one's own inner feelings, leading to the discovery and articulation of authentic moral postures.

Gilligan's criticism that Kohlberg's model of moral development is largely a male-oriented one has not held up well empirically. Research has not generally supported the notion that men tend to score higher on Kohlberg's moral scale than do women (Thoma 1986). The failure to find significant gender differences, on the other hand, does not in itself invalidate her idea that there may be two styles of moral decision-making. Based on an extensive study of what he terms *moral sensitivity*, psychologist David Loye (forthcoming) has also discovered two styles of moral decision-making.

Loye chooses the expression *moral sensitivity* because it implies more than the idea of judgment; it also points to a level of moral awareness. Loye's investigation involves intensive scholarship in three fields. The first is the historical record of human culture. Here he focuses on the cultural attractors of the Old European gylanic and subsequent domi-nator social orders discussed above. Clearly these represent divergent moral principles, and it is not hard to see in them something along the lines of Gilligan's community-oriented or caring morality on the one hand, and Kohlberg's individual justice morality on the other. Though these may be metaphorically tied to notions of the masculine and the feminine, they apparently represent a broader set of motifs in human moral sensitivity.

The second field from which Loye draws strongly is research and clinical observation concerning the brain. The findings suggest that moral sensitivity is rooted in the very biology of the human nervous system. Most helpful here were the pioneering efforts of Alexander

Luria. From Luria's careful observations of psychological losses incurred when various regions of the brain are damaged, Loye is able to articulate a surprisingly distinct set of functions performed by the brain in appraising new situations and making plans to deal with them. One of these functions turns out to be moral sensitivity. That there is a biological foundation for moral sensitivity should not, perhaps, be surprising. Loye points out that precursors of human moral behavior can be found throughout the natural world, from symbiosis between single-celled organisms through cooperative interactions in many species of higher animals (Augros and Stanciu 1987, 1992).

The third area that Loye scrutinizes is the literature of previous scientific analyses of moral behavior. Here, he finds that, prior to Kohlberg, two distinct patterns of moral behavior had been discovered. These fit remarkably well with the two motifs already described. One emphasized individual right behavior, while the other stressed compassion, nurturance, and caring. These two motifs were described in one form or another by Marx and Engels (Engels 1972), in Piaget's (1965) studies of the moral development of children, in the writings of Wilhelm Reich (1972), in the intellectuals of the Frankfurt School (Jay 1973), and in the work of Erich Fromm (1947).

It would seem from all of the above that the two major cultural attractors, which we have identified with the gylanic and dominator social orders, correspond to two fundamentally disparate moral dispositions. These are the Gilligan and Kohlberg orientations. At their highest octave, they each bring the authentic inclinations of the individual into direct relationship and even confrontation with traditional cultural values. On the other hand, there is a tendency for the Kohlberg orientation to lead to a dogged insistence on particular moral attitudes in the face of all opposition. Such commitment is no doubt admirable in and of itself, but in a world of cultural cross-currents and social transformation it can be out of place and dangerous.

It is to be hoped that the new flexibility associated with a postmodern release from rigid perspectival maps will provide a field for the agile interplay of these modes, combining the strength and commitment of the one with the compassion and contextual appropriateness of the other.

Having examined the role of cognitive maps in the life of the individual, the following chapters will turn to an exploration of the evolutionary origins of such maps, and then to their role in human history. Finally, we will examine the potential that the understanding of such maps allows for a better world of the future.

CHAPTER TWO

The Cognitive Maps of Societies

In the first chapter of this book, we explored the importance of cognitive maps in the lives of individual human beings, the role they play in creating each person's unique reality, and the role they play in guiding social and moral behavior. All of this was seen from the perspective of the individual and his or her experience of the world, an experience intensely colored by the nature of his or her own cognitive maps. From this perspective we also examined the nature of human culture, finding in it a construction, a patchwork, of individual cognitive maps. More than this, however, it is a patchwork that emerges as a force in its own right, influencing the lives of individuals as surely as its own substance was woven originally from the maps of those individual human beings.

In the present chapter we return again to an examination of the fabric of social cognitive maps, but this time from a different perspective. Here, we emphasize the influence of society on the individual, rather than the other way round, thus bringing into context the enormously important influence of culture as history, evolving as a living dynamic system that carries in tow the lives of individual human beings.

The Swiss psychiatrist Carl Jung devoted much of his life to the study of powerful collective images, which he termed *archetypes*. He showed beyond reasonable doubt that these represent important determinants of the unconscious life of the modern human (Jung 1961). According to Jungian theory, such archetypes are projected outward on to other people, and on to society as a whole. Indeed, from Jung's perspective, a great deal of what is taken for granted, in both one's internal and external worlds, is formatted by projections of archetypal images. In later years, Jung became particularly concerned about the power of archetypes to pattern the realities of entire societies. For instance, he felt that the rise of the Third Reich represented the ascendance, at the level of an entire nation, of what he called the *Odin archetype*, the image of ruthlessness and conquest. On a more positive note, in one of his last works, he speculated that widespread reports of flying saucers in the late 1940s and the 1950s were brought about by the collective influence of the *self*, the central archetype of the personality (Jung 1959).

Jung believed that archetypes gradually develop over long spans of human history. Recent scientific speculations that bear on the question of collective images suggest, however, that they may have the potential to develop considerably more rapidly (Sheldrake 1987; Laszlo 1987b, 1995). Laszlo (1993), for instance, has shown how the patterns of thought and behavior of even a single person might become the source of a formative influence, potentially available as a gentle patterning force on other persons, even in the future. This notion, which he calls the *psi-effect*, is rooted in contemporary quantum physics. It postulates that mathematical wave functions controlling the fate of individual subatomic particles are built up into increasingly higher-order or *nested* structures that have a direct influence on complex real-world events. In this case, such influence would be felt at the level of the neural processes in the brain. The nested quantum structures are "nonlocal," and stand beyond ordinary time as well. Such ideas are dramatically opposed to the mechanistic spirit of turn-of-the-century science prevalent when Jung was developing his original thoughts on archetypes. The realities of modern quantum physics, however, make them considerably more credible today (Combs and Holland 1990).

Evidently, cognitive maps exist on many levels. Social cognitive maps are supported by many minds acting in concert, any one of which contains only a part of an entire cultural map. At the same time, we have discovered the possibility of patterning fields that could mediate collective influences between minds themselves. A tentative conclusion regarding such fields is that they could effectively constitute subtle cognitive maps that might influence whole populations of people. It is, of course, difficult to observe such maps as pure instances beyond the rich surrounding influence of ongoing communications between individuals. Indeed, it is precisely the nesting of such collective maps within the buzz of ordinary discussion that seems to amplify their effectiveness. When the world's stock markets take a dip, or a regional or global recession sets in, a variety of levels of communication immediately become active. These range from many sorts of electronic transmissions to conversations carried on over lunch. The atmosphere of the event, however, seems larger, more foreboding, than the sum of the bits of information transmitted in all of these ongoing channels.

We must evidently enlarge our concept of culture to include not only the overlapping projections of individual cognitive maps, but the possibility of the projections of collective ones. One implication of all this is that collective maps carry the culture forward into the future with a greater momentum than the cumulative effects of individual maps could muster. The spirit of an age, for example, is more than an abstracted description of the general themes and individual experiences that characterize it. It is a collective map that embodies the unique themes of that particular moment in history. In terms of physics, such collective maps may well represent an objective process—one that asserts itself, via the brain, on the mental life of individuals.

Of Brains and Societies

The notion of social cognitive maps implies an analogy between social systems and brains, whether human or otherwise. It is problematic enough to suppose that what happened in the brain of a rat running through mazes in Tolman's laboratory is equivalent to what happens in a human brain flying an airplane or writing a book, but at least the two organisms have physiological material in common. There are no neurons in societies, no eyes or ears, no speech centers or limbic systems. How then can we claim that societies establish representations that orient them in space and guide their behavior in time?

Of course, the analogy has to be approximate. For the sake of convenience, the term *cognitive map* is being used to refer to both personal and public representations, and this may lead to some confusion. The analogy, however, is not as preposterous as it may initially seem, and terminological symmetry can have certain advantages. The name we apply to a phenomenon influences how we think about it, and the search for underlying unities implied by a universal term may lead to valuable insights.

To begin with, let us just think about a few facts. It is true, for instance, that children understand their parents, even in the midst of so-called "youth rebellions." The mere fact that generations can share a common language indicates that behavioral skills can be passed on pretty much uncorrupted from one period of time to another. Parents and children may not agree on much at given moments. Nevertheless, they tend to agree about which programmed response is appropriate to a shared experience, and do it using the same words (Connerton 1989; Fentress and Wickham 1992).

More dramatic examples abound, some of them seemingly trivial, but all instructive. What these examples tend to demonstrate is that collective, social realities actually do exist; that a new level of reality does emerge with human social systems. Organized human entities like teams, fire fighters, or military units are as real as biological individuals. In all of these organisms, a system-level reality has emerged. They each acquire, store, and process environmental information on the organizational level. In them, what happens to one happens to all, and the society acting as a whole can solve problems individuals cannot solve for themselves. Individual interests are subordinated to collective goals, and individual accomplishments transcend private skill. No player on a team, for instance, can advance to a world championship—no matter what his or her skill—if the team is defeated.

The firemen who raced into the burning nuclear reactor at Chernobyl had no biological advantage and little individual interest in what they were doing. In fact, most of them fully realized that by entering the plant they were exposing themselves to levels of radiation that would inevitably prove fatal. It is doubtful that many of them would have entered the blazing structure if left to themselves, just as men in combat will flee once their unit identity has been shattered after attrition rates approach a third. But in disasters, team sports, and wars, men are not alone. Nor are they acting on biological impulses. They will do what their society wants for as long as they believe that their society continues to exist.

In sport, disasters, and war, people are members of social systems. Those systems redefine their biological components, giving them attributes they do not have individually. In games, players may run faster or move more quickly; in disasters, firemen may sacrifice themselves with great nobility; in war, solders may kill with "inhuman" viciousness. On their own, athletes may be only moderately well coordinated, and they are never as much fun to watch in practice as in games. Firemen may be as reluctant to pay taxes individually as junk bond salesmen. And in their barracks soldiers may be only marginally harder to get along with than civilians. But during games, in crises, or in battle, all these people will display characteristics that are functions of their social identities, not their biological, or psychological, selves.

As members of societies, people will do to varying degrees what the social system wants, not what they want to do themselves. The things people do constitute what a social system is, and if successive generations of people display a characteristic set of distinguishing behaviors it is fair to say that the social system is a self-organized, or autopoietic, system. Society "knows" how to do certain things, and it will "teach" those things to young people as they replace their elders in approved social roles, in the same way that replicating cells in a biological organism learn to be parts of livers or kidneys or brains.

It is hard for us to recognize the emergent level of a social process, for we are observing social systems from the perspective of just one of their parts. The mere fact that we do not recognize the existence of a social brain, therefore, is no more significant than the (presumed) fact that an individual neuron does not know it is part of a biological brain—let alone that it, the separate neuron, is having a great idea! We can see evidence that something is going on, however, from history as well as from an average person's point of view.

Perhaps the best place to begin is with technology. Technology is one of the ways that every society perceives its environment, but its form varies wildly from place to place and time to time. Moreover, we tend to associate it with individual inventiveness and skill. So technology should be an example of how social systems change, rapidly and significantly because of innovations in their basic organs of perception.

But V. Gordon Childe (1951), the Australian archaeologist who rattled so many academic cages, noticed that there are, of course, many ways to form a crude stone implement, and that people in different places and at different times have tried many of them. In fact, people at different times in the same place used different techniques to produce stone tools, weapons, and artifacts. But at any one time, he discovered to his surprise, all the manufactured implements in a particular location are made in exactly the same way. At any given level of any particular dig only one technique for manufacturing is ever discovered. The homogeneity of chosen methods suggests that a social group has a shared, approved procedure for manufacture, and that every youth raised in its bosom will be taught that technique and discouraged from exploring others.

Making implements is a behavior that requires knowledge of an environment and the skills needed to survive in it. People have to know whether to use flint or sandstone in making an ax, whether to flake or grind it, and how to use the ax in gaining food. No individual in a single lifetime is likely to be able to discover that axes made from stone collected at some particular spot can be used to hunt a certain kind of game in another spot later in the year. This kind of knowledge is accumulated over long periods of time, probably with a high degree of trial and error, through the observations of many people. Somehow they have to share that knowledge.

But when knowledge is shared something wonderful and not immediately obvious happens—people are thinking in each other's brains. The effects can be quite spectacular. An Aboriginal Australian, for example, can travel from one end of the continent to the other without ever being lost, despite the fact that he may never previously have wandered more than a few miles from his birth place (Chatwin 1988). He can do that because he has received, with the social equivalent of his mother's milk, knowledge gained by generations of explorers. During a "walkabout," the native Australian is guided by the experiences of people who may have died centuries earlier and whose lives were spatially remote. But the record of what they saw and learned can be passed on to him, and the contemporary walker has virtually the same experiences as the ancestors during the Dreamtime lost in history.

When people can think in one another's brains, it is obvious that the constraints of physics, chemistry, and biology are being transcended; that, in fact, a new level of reality has emerged. How that process happened exactly is unknown and unknowable. But we can speculate with reasonable intelligence about it, at least in general terms. But just because we are forced by the absence of historical documentation to think on a general level, we need not lose an appreciation for the distinctly individual flavor of Sumerian or Egyptian or Mayan civilization.

As we have shown in Chapter 1, human societies have their origins in biological capacities that people share with other animals. But it is clear that human societies represent differences in kind from the groups and societies of other creatures. They are more tightly organized than herds of cattle and more flexible than insect colonies. So the questions for us have to begin with why and how human societies emerged in their peculiar forms. The lessons derived from studying self-organization in the rest of nature suggest that human action triggered a series of positive-feedback loops that, eventually, transformed the nature of human action.

Working together in loosely coupled, small groups, people, we may suppose, released some energy flow that drove an aggregate of human individuals through some critical barrier, at which point a bunch of "yous" and "mes" became an "us." That critical boundary would involve increasing population supported by greater energy resources produced by domesticating animals, agriculture, new technology, and improved communication media. According to Denise Schmandt-Besserat (1986), the critical stage was reached about 8000BCE in Asia Minor, when settled agricultural communities reached populations of about 350 people. It is after this point that the first artificial "tokens" were created.

Artificial tokens are important because they indicate the need to communicate information over macroscopic distances, significant periods of time, and in large amounts. People were no longer living in such small numbers and in such close proximity that each of them knew what the others were doing by direct contact. Moreover, in a sedentary agricultural society supported by specialized technical skills, people had become more dependent upon one another; they had reached a point where whatever happened to one happened to all.

In these circumstances, a social whole emerged, a system literally greater than the sum of its human parts. From now on, things would have to be done for the good of the system, upon the survival of which depended the survival of its members. Farmers would have to irrigate fields, plant seeds, and harvest crops even when they personally would have preferred lounging around lazily. Soldiers would have to fight and die at great distances from home for "rational" causes in which they had little or no emotional stake. New classes of political, military, economic, and spiritual leaders emerged, who took profits and benefits for collective accomplishments vastly disproportionate to their personal contributions. Humanity had stepped out of nature, entering into an artificial environment where an affluent minority coerced the impoverished majority to work for the collective good.

This dramatic symmetry-break with prehistoric developments was recorded in a great variety of myths, whose attractiveness continues to lure Rousseauistic thinkers to this day. But it seems clear that, like it or not, the Edenic garden was lost irretrievably. We can continue to wax poetic about how relationships in this earlier time were superior to those of the present, how people lived closer to nature, how much more respect for the land the ancients displayed. But the more we wallow in this sort of romanticism, the more inconceivable the leap to civilization appears (Schmookler 1984). Why would these noble savages ever have left the garden? Why were they foolish enough to create societies that were hierarchical, unequal, coercive, and militaristic?

The disconcerting answer, of course, may be that people did not organize civilized societies—the societies organized themselves. Like every other step up the evolutionary ladder, civilized societies did not ask the existing life-forms for permission to punctuate the established equilibrium and create a new level of reality. Rather, nature simply took the available resources—biological humans speaking languages and using specialized tools—and mixed them together. In François Jacob's

(1982) terms, also embraced by Claude Lévi-Strauss, nature is a *tinkerer* that works by *bricolage*. Evolution is not planned in advance, and whatever emerges depends upon what is available at the moment. What is available was usually developed for its own purposes, independently of everything else and with no long-term intentionality. The available is an example of what Stuart Kauffman (1993) calls *random grammars*, any sequence of information created in whatever isolated circumstances that later proves able to interact with other strings of information to interpret one another in completely unexpected forms.

But mixing the available strings of information—for example, how to make individual humans domesticate animals, plant seeds, make tools, and educate children—can produce a structure with attributes that are underdetermined by the histories of their component parts. There is nothing about the early development of human organs, for instance, that implies what their ultimate use would be. Our eyes did not incrementally, gradually, and continuously develop from rudimentary vision sensors into the miraculously refined instruments they are today. They began as parts of our primitive brains that suddenly changed their functions when other parts of the brain developed.

The same process is true of human societies, only the social process takes on an unexpected moral dimension. We make judgments about the past—for example, adoring prehistory and condemning modern civilization. That is a perfectly reasonable thing to do, but it is a consequence of civilization itself. The idealized gardens of prehistory, where people had not yet eaten of the Tree of Knowledge, are, by definition, amoral states. People are supposed to have lived in blissful self-assurance and unity with nature because they made no moral claims; they did not even know what a moral judgment was. Moral judgments are only possible after a phase change has occurred, after people have become so mutually dependent that their societies create a behavioral space in which individual actions are evaluated in terms of their public consequences. Only after the social whole upon whose survival individuals depend emerges can there be a moral judgment.

But now people are forced to make existential choices, for they must select between actions that are immediately profitable to themselves biologically and actions that are socially beneficial to the collective in the long run. The tug of self-service and self-sacrifice produced a strain that had to be overcome. No doubt, as the people being whipped in very early Sumerian clay tablets indicate, many individuals failed to make the socially approved choice. But their actions were no longer strictly private and biological. Nor were human actions merely evaluated at the collective level; emergent social wholes possessed negative-feedback loops quite able to enforce public judgments upon private selves. The human beings through whom societal negative-feedback loops operated had to be convinced to swing their whips. Slave-drivers were almost as cruelly exploited as the driven slaves. It was the moral authority of social systems that inspired some people to coerce others.

Morality, Maps, and Social Reality

The point of the discussion above is to introduce a major idea, namely that morality is the language in which social cognitive maps are expressed. This does not come as a surprise, since the importance of moral cognitive maps was discussed in Chapter 1. Here, however, we consider the role of morality not in terms of the moral behavior of individuals, but in terms of the fabric of society itself.

Just as we cannot describe everything that happens in chemistry in terms of physics, or everything that happens in biology in terms of chemistry, we cannot describe everything in society in terms of biology. Moral maps are needed to represent emergent reality on the social level, a reality that cannot be reduced to the language of physics, chemistry, or even biology. We have to describe the collective reality of social systems in the symbolic languages used by the people who make up the systems.

When the social level of reality emerges, a public, linguistic domain is created by shared information. Suspended in that public domain, people can know things of which they have no direct experience, the way an Aboriginal can know the distant reaches of Australia without having traveled to them. Other people's bodies are providing our "sixth senses." But henceforth people can only know things in terms of linguistically shaped perceptions; they will never again experience reality unadorned and unprocessed.

Two things are critical here. First is the simple fact that to communicate information it has to be encoded and decoded. If I want you to know about my red Ferrari, I will not give you direct experience of it by driving into you with it but will say the word *Ferrari*. That word is essentially arbitrary. It has nothing to do with automobiles. It will not carry you to Portofino, attract members of the opposite sex, consume a nonrenewable resource, or pollute the atmosphere. You cannot polish the word *Ferrari* or act out fantasies driving it. But my use of the word may well excite your envy and resentment (if you had a red Ferrari, I would probably be envious and resentful). That is, despite its arbitrary nature, the word *Ferrari* entering your brain will be decoded as a representation of a sleek, powerful, expensive automobile. Through the use of an agreed code, you and I can share information. But what we share is not the Ferrari. We share the socially conditioned experience of what *Ferrari* means, and we can never experience an actual Ferrari independently of its socially determined meanings.

Secondly, with the emergence of societies, new kinds of information came to be communicated. It was no longer merely a matter of my telling you something about my experiences. In a society it is necessary to communicate information about our experience. Assuming that all our verbal pictures are designed to map the world, the emergence of societies marks a symmetry-break in which a new world has to be mapped. It is a world created when the natural environment is transformed by collective action. No aggregate of individual cognitive maps can represent the collective environment, for the social world is a whole greater than the sum of its parts. A way to encode information about the reality that transcended biology had to be found if even bricolage were successfully to find a way to glue people together into new wholes by communicating information about what happened to closely coupled social systems.

It is not irrational to suggest as an axiom that society constitutes a new level of reality, for it is perfectly reasonable to suppose that our ancestors acted cooperatively to affect their environment. Cooperation is not uncommon in prehuman species. All we need to suppose is that by cooperation our precivilized ancestors created positive-feedback loops with the environment. The result would be a release of energy that drove early human groups through a cascade of bifurcations until they self-organized into stable states that were, in part, decoupled from their original, natural environments. At that point, society could be readily distinguished from nature.

No doubt the first societies were relatively simple, which is one aspect that so endears them to Hippies. A simple system models its environment, as Bateson (1972) pointed out. But one definition of a complex system is that it also contains a model of itself (Nicolis 1986). The earliest societies of which any symbolic record remains have *cosmogenic* myths. That is, they have symbolic representations of their world and how it came to be. But it is interesting that only later do societies have *origin* myths, stories of how the people came to be. The cosmogenic myth is a representation of the world; the origin myth is a representation of a society in its world. Simple groups were models of their environments, but civilized societies were complex enough to have models of themselves. Since it takes time for the latter to be created after the former, we can postulate that social evolution involves increasing complexity in human history, as it does in the rest of nature.

In both the cosmogenic and origin myths, a people talk to themselves about their shared experiences. It is this discussion that reveals the social corollary of cognitive mapping. As we still consider how an environment is represented and how problems are to be solved in that environment, the term *cognitive map* remains appropriate. But we no longer talk about the environment experienced by individual biological creatures (Lynch 1960). Therefore, the cognitive map can no longer be recorded in the "wetware" of a brain; it can no longer be written in the "language" of biological cells or their electrochemical connections. We are now talking about the environment experienced as a result of cooperative human effort, and of the forces released by that effort into a social whole (Downs and Stea 1973; Gladwin 1970).

Collective Experience, Myths, and Maps

Respecting the fact that a social cognitive map must be encoded in symbolic human languages replete with moral terms, we can give the following definition: a *societal cognitive map* is the set of shared symbols describing a collective environment and prescribing the organized behaviors appropriate to preserving social stability in that environment. In its descriptions a societal cognitive map locates the principle physical aspects of the environment—mountains, valleys, rivers, etc. (Frankfort 1973). These descriptions are rarely in terms that moderns recognize as "scientifically" valid, but they are usually amazingly perceptive and often better informed than the modern white Westerners who ridiculed ancient cognitive maps.

Take the Sumerian cosmogenic myth as an example. It tells the story of how the world was delivered from the Earth Goddess after she was raped by the Wind God. Now obviously, the tale as we have it includes some later emendations. But while their sexist dominating attitudes can be decried, the validity of the basic representation cannot be disputed. The story reveals that the meanderings of the Tigris and Euphrates rivers outline a woman's body, that the wind blows off the Persian Gulf between the mouths of the two rivers, and that the heavy silt carried by the rivers builds up at a very rapid pace. Ur, for instance, was a coastal town when the story was created, but is now over two hundred miles inland.

The use of divine symbols and the attribution to the divinities of animal lusts made Sumerian cosmogony appear irrational to "scientifically" minded Westerners. But the creators of the tale accurately described their territory, provided one knew how to decode the information communicated. Westerners who did not know how to read the tales laughed at them. However, Western geographers knew less about the course of the two rivers than the ancients until British intelligence flights over the area in World War II photographed it carefully. Only when an officer who happened to be an Oxbridge orientalist laid out the pictures on a plotting board could the wisdom of the ancients finally be appreciated.

Egyptian cosmogony is similar in kind but radically different in detail. That is because the environment Egyptians had to map socially was radically different from that of Sumer. In Egypt, the Nile provides a narrow ribbon of fertile green slashed from the barren desert. Naturally enough, Egyptians described the world as a sort of celery-dish. In addition to the rains that fall sideways—the Nile—the most dominant feature of the Egyptian environment is the Sun, who became the principal god once the empire was created. The Sun was the god of Heliopolis, now only a minor city near Cairo. But once the empire was united, the priests at Memphis blended Re, the Sun, with Amon, the Air God of Memphis, to produce Amon-Re, the father of the pharaoh. It follows that this god was dominant, for, after all, a social cognitive map is the record of collective experience. Once civilization and male domination became complete, Egyptians could even imagine the male Sun God producing the world by masturbating it into existence (Reilly 1980). But even in early versions, it is the power of the Sun that draws the Earth out of the primeval waters, perfectly describing the sight of hillocks covered with fresh silt appearing to rise as the annual flood recedes.

Compared to Sumer, Egypt offered a benign environment. The land between the Tigris and Euphrates was washed by highly irregular floods, had been exposed to foreign invasion, and was sustainable only by continuous labor. The Nile, on the other hand, flowed with a notable regularity and predictability, providing virtually the same floods at virtually the same time for millennia. Its currents permitted easy travel by boat downstream, while the winds sweeping gently down the valley from the Mediterranean cooled the land and made sail-powered travel up-river almost effortless. The surrounding desert protected Egypt from attack. The result was a civilization so attractive that it was nearly heaven, which is why the Egyptians were so fascinated with the afterlife and so concerned to be prepared for it. The next world would be as perfect as this one, and all the clothes, chariots, tools, and artifacts used in Egypt would be appropriate there.

The harsh and unforgiving world of Sumer, by contrast, described its quality of life in negative terms. People were created by gods, for instance, because the gods were unwilling to toil eternally, hauling mud to clear irrigation channels or build dams. The work was thankless, since floods washed everything away in a flash or else drought left the fields to die, and only slaves could be forced to carry it out. Human beings were, therefore, the slaves of the gods, and the statues created in Sumer, bowed persons with prayerful hands and big frightened eyes, reveal the sense people had of their precarious, ever-threatened existence.

By describing people as well as places, social cognitive maps are representing collective experience. They are preserving a memory of the world experienced by the ancestral founders of a society. At the same time, by exploring what a human life means and what its worth is, social cognitive maps also prescribe the behaviors necessary for society to survive. They filter out vital information and stimulate learned responses to it. Value symbols prescribe behavior, and behavior creates social structure. Values excite emotional responses to particular persons, places, or actions. Values decide that a person is noble or craven, that a place is holy or cursed, that an action is moral or immoral. Young people are encouraged to emulate behavior that is noble and repudiate behavior that is craven, to travel to the holy places annually and avoid the cursed ones, and to replicate useful actions and eschew wasteful ones.

When successive generations tell themselves the same stories, which describe the same environment and excite the same behaviors, a complex society comes into being. Society is a model of an environment that did not exist until collective human effort created it. Precivilized peoples, no doubt, affected their environments, but the moral grandeur in which contemporary critics cloak the ancients depends upon their not having devastated the world in which they lived. Notwithstanding tales of slash-and-burn agriculture to the contrary, the point is that precivilized peoples left a limited mark upon the earth because they were not able to affect it more drastically. Wandering in small, loosely coupled bands, they lived off nature's bounty. To be sure, when their populations rose, even small bands could seriously tax a locality. But when such local resources became hard to get, the early human bands fragmented and searched for new places to forage (Mann 1986). Plant and animal life left behind in the abandoned territory could recover rapidly.

In these original bands, people are likely to have served their separate biological needs, taking as much interest in the group as cattle or birds take in herds or flocks. Group and biological individual benefited from each other, but to such a limited degree that disintegration was not a major concern. But when people began to work closely together to domesticate animals and plant crops, they created an artificial environment. The primeval forests could be mapped by the brains of individuals humans; but the artificial worlds created by collective human effort were more multi-dimensional and dynamic than the environments presented by nature. The information about a human-made environment could not all be stored in an individual brain. Nor could an individual brain anticipate the dynamics of a new environment or control collective responses. When complex societies emerged from precivilized bands, they were wholes whose survival demanded the preservation of collective behavior.

To survive, social wholes had to create means of distributing responsibility for information-processing. Everyone in a given society had to learn to speak the same language, perceive the same realities, value the same responses, internalize the same behaviors. Then, in reality, everyone could act as if they knew what the others were doing: behaviors became correlated. Individual cognitive maps cannot produce these tightly coupled correlations, for there is no way to distribute the programs for information-processing. But our precivilized ancestors found a way to act together to change their environment, to stabilize the structures cooperative action created, and rapidly to communicate information about environmental changes by mapping the world created by collective action. Moreover, because social cognitive maps are written in symbolic languages, they are uniquely suited for distribution throughout a population of human brains (Craik 1943).

Maps, Songs, and Writing

A social cognitive map is a song sung by every member of a stabilized society. The Homeric poems that mapped Greece during its "Dark Ages" were literally sung, as were the legends Pacific Islanders used to navigate the open seas. By singing the same song, members of a society are locating the same key environmental elements and triggering the behaviors necessary for the replication of the society in the future. That is, each generation learns from the song what game is available and how to hunt it, what crops to plant and where to plant them, what campsite to use and how to find it. Members of societies also learn how to relate to one another from their shared cognitive maps. When the same foods are produced and eaten by people acting out the same behaviors, the same society has been reconstituted. So, in effect, social cognitive maps are equivalent to DNA, which itself is a kind of encoded representation of an organism that represents an environment. Only now it is not the biological features of people that are being replicated. Rather, it is behavior patterns, based upon trained perceptions and excited by values shared on the collective level, that are being replicated.

A society's fitness is determined by its social cognitive map. Thus, by introducing the concept of social cognitive maps we can provide a logical explanation of human social evolution. A society survives when the description and prescriptions encoded in its cognitive map match its environment. Then the group is able to reproduce itself in competition with other groups. In other words, when people are brought up to see the world in a certain way, they survive if the world they encounter as adults is, at least within limits, as they expected. Similarly, people survive because the skills they were provided with as children prove useful in the world they exploit as adults. Finally, competing groups will be selected for or against depending upon how much of the environment they can adequately map and how relatively effective their orchestrated responses are. The group mapping more of the world and processing the information more efficiently will have an advantageous differential rate in reproducing itself and its products.

But if people are, for example, trained to hunt bears where there are no bears, or trained to worship gods too weak to defend them, their society will usually disintegrate. The map they have inherited does not match their territory and they are lost. This is an important consequence of the social cognitive map theory, for it indicates that societies are, as Childe (1951) pointed out, less adaptive than we sometimes think. It is probably true that cultural evolution is faster than biological evolution; but that is because words are cheaper than genes. We can explore the possible advantages of changing a cognitive map by manipulating word-symbols. If the members of our society approve of some metaphorical deviation, it will be endorsed and the society will evolve.

But it is less easy to change social cognitive maps in practice than it is in theory, especially after societies have become complex. Once cooperative human action has created a dynamic, multi-dimensional environment, the society embedded in it is unstable. Any fluctuation in its internal structure can reduce its capacity to process the vast amounts of environmental energy, matter, and information flowing through the society. Besides, if what we are trained to experience is what we do experience, then we may not even be conscious of altered possibilities—an ear trained to hear one kind of song may not even realize that the noise assaulting it is music! Unless a sense datum is capable of being processed by symbolic representation, it is ignored or repressed.

Of course, one reason societies do not change readily is that they have negative-feedback loops, institutionalized subsystems that model a remembered environment. Complex societies even have subsystems designed to preserve established organization by suppressing deviations. These subsystems, of which the Inquisition and the FBI are typical examples, are triggered by the values in a social cognitive map. Medieval people were encouraged to love God and obey His earthly representatives, and anti-papal heretics who deviated were sometimes burned. Americans were required to hate communists, and those who were even mildly sympathetic were followed, spied on, fired from their jobs, and frequently arrested. Burning or harassing fellow human beings must be hard work, but dedicated disciples of the Church and the American Way of Life risked their souls and mental health because they were so enamored of a particular social system that they were inflamed by any opposition to it. Inflaming those repressive passions is a way for societies to preserve their identities.

Social cognitive maps, in other words, not only teach people how to experience the world and what parts of the world to experience, but also form patterned responses to experiences. Societies sense or perceive their artificial environment through people and tools. But they shape both the people and the tools, so that they are effective filters for sorting through the "bloomin' buzzin' confusion" of external reality. There was nothing wrong with the eyes of precivilized nomads or with the noses of preindustrial Arabs. Biologically, their eyes and noses were the same as ours. Yet the nomads never exploited the agricultural resources of the river valleys and the Arabs paid no attention to the treasury of oil. Neither nomads nor Arabs were socially equipped to see the potential of these environments. Their social cognitive maps could not process the energy flows represented by irrigated agriculture or oil, so for them, in a very real sense, neither the valleys nor the oil fields existed. They were not part of the collective myth, so they were not real. Nor could the agricultural or industrial resources of river valleys and oil fields be perceived, since cooperative human action had not created the environment in which their potentials were societal actualities.

When societies perceive key features of their external environments and orchestrate responses to them, they are to all intents and purposes "thinking," as anthropologist Mary Douglas (1986) says. Of course, societies do not think by illuminating neural networks, for they are not made of neural networks. They are made of individuals and subsystems or "institutions." Societies think by activating organized programs for dealing with perceived problems by energizing institutions. When, for instance, strangely costumed foreigners approach a society's boundaries and a specialized class of comparably costumed males march out to give battle, society is thinking. It has perceived a change in its environment and responded by activating a prepared program previously shown to be effective. And it should be admitted that, by going to war, society as a whole is solving problems its individual members cannot solve for themselves.

Societies remember which behaviors solved problems in the past by storing information. Information is stored in a variety of ways. The most obvious are written documents, but they came late. Preliterate bands recorded their experiences through rituals and sung myths (Goody 1977; Turner 1986). Modern anthropologists notice a peculiar quality to the mythical life of preliterate groups: they do not take their rituals and myths lightly; it is not enough for them to attend church for an hour on Sunday and ignore religion the rest of the week. Preliterate peoples, we are told, live in their rituals and myths. That is, by performing a ritual or singing a mythic tale, preliterate peoples are actually acting out the divine adventure they describe. By doing so, they recreate both the cosmos and the people in the present.

Ritual and myth, therefore, are not merely ways of remembering past experiences; they are techniques for structuring present behaviors in exact imitation of the remembered past, which is literally present in the ritual or myth. Ritual and myth transport information from the past to the present, and, by the religious reenactment, those behaviors are replicated in the present. Ritual and myth are able to replicate the people whose behaviors preserve the rituals and myths as surely as successful mating songs reproduce flocks of birds. Ritual and myths, the earliest forms of social cognitive maps, act as DNA, which is how societies endure over time.

Of course, advanced biological brains think by creating new ideas, which societies do as well. A new social idea is a new behavioral role, and when societies create ideas they "make up new people," in Ian Hacking's phrase (1985). The prophet, the poet, the philosopher, and the physicist are all identities that are not found in nature, or even in preliterate societies. They are specialized identities produced in response to enriched environments that cannot be read through the prism of a monolithic social role. New social roles imply that new aspects of the environment are being perceived, for patterned individual behaviors are one method that societies have of "sensing" their worlds. By making up new people, societies do more than endure. They evolve by demonstrating that they can learn—perceive, store, and process—new information.

Most of the time, however, societies "develop" rather than "evolve." They streamline themselves by learning how to perform established tasks better. Only on rare occasions do societies learn qualitatively new tricks, break the symmetry of their historical development, and experience a discontinuous leap to levels of increased complexity. Because most laboratory examples of this fundamental evolutionary process are much quicker, it is not well understood. But perhaps the slow time scale—relative to individual lifetimes—of societal transitions can be observed more completely. Then the difficulty of translating scientific models to society can be made worthwhile, for science might end up with a better understanding of some fundamental problems. Let us begin with a modest presupposition, namely that the earliest societies were relatively crude brains. That does not mean that the brains of the individuals making up the earliest societies were crude—they were the most refined biological learning machines ever evolved, at least as far as we know.

The biological brains in the earliest societies were human brains. But the networked interdependencies connecting them were few and loose. So the reality that was emerging in the symmetry break from biological to social evolution had not progressed very far. Even the first civilized societies, whether in Sumer, Egypt, China, or America, were all thinking systems that, like frog brains, relied more on genetic than on acquired memory. They had found particular roles and relationships that effectively modeled the artificial environments created by irrigation, for example. Having found the roles and relationships suited to processing this information, societies were determined to preserve the ability. It turned out that a hierarchical structure, informed by writing, gathered in cities, and with a ceremonial center, worked best.

It was able to distribute food, tools, and weapons, repress divergent behavior, and defend frontiers.

So far as anyone knew, the structured procedures embraced by a society were the only ones capable of anticipating environmental dynamics fast enough to preserve stability. In the social cognitive maps encoding information, all these societies included cautionary tales about how bold attempts to wrest power or knowledge from the gods invited disaster. They also recalled an earlier period of formless anarchy, which was negatively valued by being made frightening. The point of all this was to teach people to worship the existing form of society and not risk its collapse by experimentation. Durkheim was right: "Society is God." And by making knowledge divine, it was protected from sacrilegious experimentation.

The first civilized states, therefore, have a kind of crystalline appearance. They may have been wealthy, productive, and artistic beyond previous measure, but they were rigid and unyielding in their attempts to preserve an identity as near to that of their ancestors as possible. It is probably true that pre-civilized societies were equally rigid—in intent. But one of the unexpected consequences of writing was that civilized societies actually were better able to achieve a fixed identity of themselves than their precivilized predecessors.

Preliterate, "aural" societies were able to preserve vast amounts of information over long periods of time. They did it, as Homer did, and as fundamentalist preachers in the American South do to this day, by using a relatively small number of phrases, messages, and metaphors that are deeply entrenched in social tradition. Consequently, a bard or storyteller can recount incredibly long tales about ancient heroes and their adventures, frequently in great detail. The repetition of familiar phrases and phrasings permits the story to go on and on.

But every telling of a story connotes a slight difference in meaning, for meaning is established by the context in which a message is decoded. It is the social environment that ultimately decodes messages. In preliterate societies, the social environment is able to drift incrementally with every slight shift in routinized experiences. Auditors of a tale, therefore, do not detect any transformation in messages as they are ritualistically repeated. There is no fixed reference against which to compare today's retelling with yesterday's original. Consequently, as the society drifts, it slightly alters its defining tales without being aware of it.

But literate societies have perfectly preserved versions of original sources. The Code of Hammurabi is carved into a stone stela, to which any literate Sumerian could easily refer. A lawyer or administrator who slightly modified the law to meet immediate contingencies, therefore, would quickly have the error of his ways pointed out—and there were written punishments for those convicted of falsifying the law. Once a legal system was preserved in written form, it could be modified only with great difficulty. Of course, it was not until societies became complex that they required writing to communicate information. But then writing had the tendency to freeze the society in a particular image. Any variation in the environment, however, would require adaptive responses. When these became difficult, societies tended to become less fitted to their environments, and hence less stable.

The Maps of the Religions

Complex civilized societies were able to survive because they created new types of cognitive map, maps able to represent dynamic social environments and to process vast flows of information. These new types of cognitive map include the "higher" religions, which, like all the cognitive maps of civilized societies, purport to be delivered to humankind from divine sources. It is this record of delivery from "on high" that is our best clue that an evolved level of reality emerged. People are recording their experience of an event which is not physical but which they nevertheless experience to the very core of their beings. This indicates a level of reality that is created by preserving collective knowledge of a shared environment in relationships that endure generation after generation. The laws delivered to Hammurabi or Moses by their respective gods on the mountain tops froze societies into rigid structural forms, any deviations from which were severely punished.

The higher religions give the impression that they came "out of the blue." But they are as much historical artifacts as the social structures with which they coevolve. In fact, it is relatively easy to read the history of the peoples who created the higher religions through their sacred documents (Fox 1992; Wilson 1992). Here we shall concentrate on the Western tradition, since that is the one which eventually departed from civilized conventions and created a new kind of cognitive map.

There are two basic roots of the Western religious tradition, Hellenism and Hebraism. These two traditions are radically opposed to one another, and it can be argued, as the German poet Heinrich Heine did, that the tension between these two opposing religious views is what gives the West its peculiar dynamism. The contrasts between Hellenic and Hebraic religiosity exist on virtually every level, with the Jews usually being given the nod for having produced the more significant version. Greek gods were fairly typical pagan deities; numerous and anthropomorphic, they often appeared to Victorian commentators as personifications of every libidinal drive on perpetual holiday. They had sexual relations with each other and with humans, their sexuality was not confined to what later Western authorities considered normal, and their lust-driven betrayals of responsibility and decorum still seem offensive. Aphrodite, for instance, was married to Hephaistos but was sleeping with Mars. (Love, in other words, betrayed Technology for War.)

The Olympian gods left much to be desired from every ethical point of view. The male sky gods dominated. Like Homer's Achilles, they took what they wanted, when they wanted it, and by any available means. The only interests they served were their own. But the male sky gods were constantly being tricked, deceived, and otherwise manipulated by female earth goddesses. Their main figure, Hera, was an obstinate, spiteful, conniving personality, who was inclined to bathe only when planning to seduce Zeus, her husband, into some action he would live to regret.

But crude though it may have been, the Greek pantheon did effectively map experience and record history. What the Homeric gods describe is a social environment formed when nomadic raiders from the north spilled into Greece riding horses—cf., the "centaurs"—and conquered an older, sedentary agricultural society. The nomads, being travelers, worshipped sky gods, who are almost always male. The Chthonians, being farmers, worshipped female earth goddesses. The rapine and pillage of conquest is symbolized in the marriage of Zeus and Hera, the nomads' god and the farmers' goddess. Their stormy celestial relationship must have perfectly mirrored the domestic situation in many Greek homes.

There was really no ethical dimension to the pagan Greek religion. It was framed by conquering aristocrats, horsemen who carried bronze weapons. These were people who valued excellence, but who felt no compulsion to curb power in the interest of good. Hesiod's *Works and Days*, the only source comparable to Homer, reinforces this idea in the litany of complaints expressed from the farmers' point of view. The aristocrats' main value—*arete*—extolled virtuosity, not virtue. It proclaimed the ideal of glory won by the display of skill, not ethical conduct. And why not, since Olympus was where the gods of conquerors dwelled. The men whose world was mapped by Homer's songs relied on their individual prowess to survive. They had no need for societal restraints to protect them. According to Homer and Hesiod, their only interest in the weak was to rob and exploit them.

By Homer's time, a mismatch between the Greek cognitive map and the environment was beginning to show. The *Iliad*, for instance, is a war poem, telling the story of a ten-year conflict to preserve Greek honor after a Trojan dandy violated the norms of aristocratic etiquette by absconding with the wife of his host. In specific descriptions, Homer details the martial prowess of his hero, the warrior Achilles. But it is clear from the spirit of the poem that Homer's real sympathies are with the Trojans, protectors of the city and its humane values. The tragedy of the *Iliad* is that the barbarians prevail, Achilles's *arete* proves victorious when linked with the amoral cunning of Odysseus.

The explanation for Homer's mixed mood, glorying in prowess but lamenting mindless destruction, is to be found in the shifting Greek environment. Homer lived about six hundred years after the nomadic conquest and well into the Greek "Dark Ages," at a time when Greece was slowly beginning to revive. Cities were again stable, and piracy was giving way to trade. The experience of Greek life was no longer adequately described by the oral tradition handed down from the days of Troy, and Homer's ordering of the verses probably reflects just the sort of incremental departure from convention that would usually go unnoticed in an aural society.

But Homer was so great a poet that he infatuated the whole of Greece with his versions of their national epoch, and pride was ever after taken in the ability to recite verbatim the poems as Homer had arranged them. Besides, it was not long after Homer's death that writing was reintroduced into Greece, making the official version hard to ignore. So, by the seventh century BCE, Greeks began to feel a certain unease as they tried to balance the needs of actual experience against the prescriptive values of tradition.

It was such creative thinkers as Thales of Miletus (?625–?547BCE) who exploited the gap between map and territory and articulated a philosophical alternative. As a merchant, Thales traveled widely, and knowledge was among the things he brought back to the *agora*, or marketplace. For example, he had seen the pyramids in Egypt and learned the skill of making a corner perfectly square. Transferring that technology proved problematic, for Thales needed an explanation for why stretching a rope with twelve equal spaces in it produced a perfect right-angled triangle. The Egyptians, of course, explained the phenomenon as a gift of their architecture god. But gods do not travel well from culture to culture, even when information does. Nor could a people who were already "more moral than their [own] gods" (Murray 1951) attribute to them an accomplishment this grand, especially since Homer had not mentioned it. So Thales invented geometry by figuring out a logical argument to demonstrate why the spatial relationships between a three–four–five triangle necessitate that the angle opposite the hypotenuse is ninety degrees.

The breakthrough to a rational, secular view of the world has often been touted as the "Greek Miracle." The Greeks deserve much credit for their creativity, but the societal cognitive map concept suggests that there was nothing miraculous about it. In fact, by searching for rational proofs or explanations, the Greeks were as clearly mapping their new, stable urban and political environment as the Sumerians or Egyptians mapped irrigated valleys with their myths. But in Greece, which came to civilization late and was influenced by foreign sources, the inherited symbolic representation was inferior to others and, in any case, no longer reflective of actual experience. Greek merchants were not the same ruthless thieves their forefathers had been, and Greek soldiers were no longer aristocratic warriors.

Greece had changed in the centuries after Homer, and the change was nowhere more apparent than in military matters. Iron technology had replaced bronze for weapon-making, and iron made weapons cheap enough for middle-class farmers and tradesmen to purchase. These people greatly outnumbered the aristocrats, and if the townsmen could organize themselves into a disciplined infantry they would be able to sweep the noble cavalry from the rock-strewn floors of the narrow valleys separating the cities. The problem was figuring out a device for integrating an infantry in which peaceful individual shopkeepers would willingly risk life and limb for the public good. Traditionally, force was the means employed to coerce cooperation. But when everyone is armed, force becomes self-destructive, and if a policy decision was reached through violence it would not be sustained during battle. An infantry unit, called the *Phalanx* in Greece, that was forced to fight a foreign invader after a civil war would hardly be efficient. Having bullied its members into combat, the Phalanx could expect to dissolve once battle started.

So the Greeks, unwittingly, invented "democracy," the technique of talking themselves into battle by openly arguing among themselves until a consensus was reached. When words rather than swords are depended upon, opinion changes because of logical persuasion. The point here is obvious. When Thales began to explain the world independently of the Greek gods as a logical structure where law controlled action, he was simply reading into nature a symbolic representation of his own political environment. And Thales knew that environment well, since he was the first statesman to perceive the Persian threat to Greece and to lobby for a defensive union between the Ionian cities. In the politicized Greek environment, men moved because of reason, and they moved with terrible efficiency, as the Persian hordes learned to their dismay. Why then should not the material elements of the physical world be similarly controlled by law and logic?

The possibility was so exciting that Greek thinkers explored its many nuances in a 150-year intellectual explosion of almost unequaled creativity. But when it was all over, Parmenides, Zeno, and Plato fairly well demonstrated the bankruptcy of the exercise. To be sure, we stand in awe of Greek "scientists" who "discovered" virtually everything from atomism to evolution. But the Greeks, who were after all still the highly competitive spiritual sons of Achilles eager for glory, were more struck by Zeno's demonstration that none of these thinkers could explain something as common as how an arrow reached its mark, or could even move. The thinkers had many arguments, and while all were persuasive none was compelling. During stable times, the leisured intellectuals could gleefully compete in public trying to shoot down each other's arguments and advance their own theories. But after the Peloponnesian Wars, in which Athens and Sparta devastated the whole peninsula, times were no longer stable. And the common person, after all, had never found much advantage in rigorously abstract, formalized demonstrations of ideas that no one could prove in practice. It is not surprising, after the middle of the fourth century BCE, either that an outsider like Alexander the Great could conquer the Greeks, or that most Greeks would begin looking for a social cognitive map that offered meaning, promise, and protection to the lives of ordinary people.

The basis of an alternative map was being forged in the hostile desert environment of the Middle East by the Hebrews, a people too few in number to conquer much of anything. They began in accordance with their sacred history as nomadic bands of shepherds organized into families and clans that each worshipped its animistic spirit. Wandering into the fertile crescent, they were marched over by a series of conquering armies and eventually taken to Egypt. After a period of several generations, they were led by Moses out of captivity and into the Promised Land. On the way they formed a covenant with the god of an extinct volcanic mountain, at the top of which they received their law.

Moses was a less effective navigator than his talk in Egypt promised, and by the time the Jews were Chosen by Yahweh they were lost and in danger of fragmenting. The Covenant with Yahweh was a critical device for ensuring loyalty, for all Jews were bound to obey the law, repudiate the syncretic tendencies inherent in their geographical position, and worship only this One God. Focusing the tribes on the One God enabled Moses and later leaders to hold society together.

But the god of Moses is hardly more edifying than those of the Greeks. He is distinctly human-like, depicted as walking through the Garden of Eden trying to find Adam and Eve. He is often spiteful, imposing arbitrary obligations such as the prohibition against eating fruit from the trees of Life and Knowledge on His followers and then punishing them for acts of disobedience the Greeks would have admired. His conduct could be capricious, as poor Job found to his dismay. And He was always suspicious, as the demand for Abraham to sacrifice Isaac indicates. But all of these traits merely indicate the kind of god a people living in the desert is likely to have invented to map their world. Their God, like the whirlwind or burning bush from which He spoke, was harsh, unpredictable, and ceaselessly demanding.

At the time of Moses, the Jews were not yet monotheistic; they were monolatrous. They worshipped only one god, but that does not indicate that they believed other gods were any the less real. However, the covenanted obligation not to worship other idols provided an opportunity for the Jews to understand the terrible things which repeatedly happened to them. They were, for instance, defeated in war and carried off into slavery in Babylon not because Yahweh was weaker than Baal, the Babylonian God, but because some Jews, tempted by syncretism, had begun offering libations and other sacrifices to the gods of a richer, more powerful people. Angered by this betrayal, Yahweh raised the Babylonian scourge as a punishment for the law-breaking Jews.

The capacity for Yahweh to change sides introduced a certain spirituality into his identity. It was never possible for a wandering people to worship at a particular spot or cart about a heavy totem, but as Yahweh tracked the experiences of his people he acquired an ever more intangible quality. Building on this development, the prophets in Exile—who still had the problem of holding together a society without territorial boundaries—took an even bolder step. If Yahweh's power raised the Babylonians against Israel as just punishment for violating the Covenant, then there was no need for Baal at all. He was superfluous. In fact, argued Isaiah, there is really only one God, and that God is pure spirit and universal.

A purely spiritual, universal, single god is usually taken as representing the "higher" religions. But the Jews had even more to offer, for in their law they also introduced the concept of ethics. Unlike the Homeric Greeks, the Jews did not do things because they could, which would have been limiting indeed, given their environmental circumstances; they did things because they were good. It was virtue, not virtuosity, that Yahweh demanded. The poor and weak, the homeless and downtrodden, the orphaned and widowed, all these were groups that Jews were morally bound not only to respect, but to help. Again, it is obvious (as Nietzsche suggested) that these ideas should map the experiences of a small, frequently conquered and politically weak people. Ethics sheathed the sword of the powerful in Israel, just as democratically rooted nationalism reduced the propensity for discord among the middle-class members of the Phalanx in Greece. In either case, a value symbol was developed for reducing internal social violence.

But the ancient Jews were not interested in reducing violence between themselves and other peoples. On the contrary, their brief period of political independence and cultural dominance under King David and his heirs wet the Hebrew appetite to own their own territory and control their own destiny. The prophets assured them that, sticking strictly to the letter of the law, God would reward them with a Messiah or Savior who would carve out an empire for them.

Unfortunately, the rising Roman star was destined to eclipse Jewish political ambitions by a series of increasingly bloody, ruthless repressions. But just as the Greeks were able to adapt the Homeric value of *arete* from its original militaristic expression and moderate it into an intellectual skill in debate, members of the Jewish community began to explore other meanings of the term "Messiah." If it could not prove functional in political and military terms against superior Roman strength, perhaps it could acquire a spiritual and ethical meaning. Groups like the Essenes, who authored the Dead Sea Scrolls, began to search for a style of life that would lead to identity and community on a higher plane than politics.

It seems probable that Christ emerged out of this environment, and his teachings were a mapping of a transformed Romanized world using the language of Hebrew tradition. Perhaps the most fundamental need his ideas addressed were the sense of purposelessness and alienation typical of the Hellenistic age. All over the Mediterranean world, Rome was restoring peace. But it was a peace established only after two centuries of civil war had demonstrated the bankruptcy of republican institutions. What emerged in the Roman Empire—the same as in the

Alexandrian empire—was a bureaucratized society, governed from afar by managers with little knowledge of, and even less interest in, local affairs. There seemed no alternative to this solution, since only Roman power could establish law. Moreover, dictatorial or not, the Roman Empire ushered in two hundred years of prosperity from which most classes benefited.

But it must have been extremely difficult for men raised in the traditions of Achilles and Cincinnatus to yield dominion over their lives to emperors, generals, and bureaucrats. Seneca, whose high ethical ideals and republican sentiments could not control the power of Nero or abate its arbitrary exercise, fell on his sword. His suicide demonstrated the old Roman values in their noblest form—and their ineffectuality. To more average people, the situation was even worse. They lived in peace and plenty, fed bread and entertained by circuses. But they lived in an immense state over which they had no control and which was ruled for the benefit of a handful of military and civilian authorities.

People really cannot live by bread alone, at least not once their personalities have been transformed by the evolution of social complexity; they must have some sense of moral worth and purpose. But that comes from the match between their social cognitive map and their environment. When the match breaks down, people are confused, lost, and alienated, as they were in the Mediterranean when Alexander arose, and later with the ascendance of the Romans. People who had come to think of themselves in terms of their contribution to their cities, and who were responsible for their own actions, now had decisions made for them. They experienced the effects of external decisions over which they had no control.

The upper-class Greek response to this was suitably philosophical. The Cynics proclaimed the artificiality of all conventions and vowed to live like dogs as they searched for virtue. The Epicureans advised that the search be limited to a carefully controlled garden, populated with a few friends. And the Stoics proclaimed that, although there was a universal law, few of us ever got a glimpse into it or could predict its effects. All these schools, and the rhetoricians who proclaimed that truth was relative, were recording the experiences of people living in a world they could not map. The less articulate masses founded no schools, but in the resurrection of ancient chthonic fertility rites and the invention of new miracle religions they expressed a comparable sense that the Roman world held nothing of value for them—an escape to greener pastures was desirable.

There were, however, no greener pastures in this world—Rome had gobbled up all of them. But Rome had offered no spiritual benefits into the bargain. It had not even seriously undertaken to map its own reality cognitively. To be sure, a fair number of poets, including Virgil, had volunteered to cloak the imperial power in a robe of mythic authority. But while the *Aeneid* could extol the virtues of obedience, authority, and family, even its beauty could not conceal the intellectual vacuum behind the Roman purple. Augustus had made himself first citizen in name, but was emperor in fact. He knew Roman conservatism would never countenance an overt departure from tradition, so he hid his iron fist in the velvet glove of embalmed republican institutions. To complete the public-relations campaign behind which he grasped every lever of power absolutely, Augustus lived in humble housing, wore clothes of home-spun cloth, ate camp food, and held his family to puritanical standards.

Augustus's false advertising made Rome look as if it was still a republic, although, as Caligula's decision to make himself a god demonstrates, Augustus had made Rome an empire in the conventional civilized sense. But what his policies did was to force Rome to live a lie—clinging to the illusion of a rural republican virtue, the Romans felt themselves living the reality of imperial cosmopolitanism. They could not govern a universal empire on the basis of auguries and omens, but they would not repudiate the faith of their ancestors. So there was no map of the Roman territory, and despite the prosperity, people increasingly defined themselves as "corrupt." They began to look elsewhere for spiritual guidance. Christ's teachings were among the many possibilities they considered.

At first, it was mostly the poor, the enslaved, and the illiterate who rallied to the Christian message. Only the most alienated and helpless could have found it appealing. After all, Christ was a despised Jew, whose fellow countrymen were still rebelling against Rome. Unlike most Gods, he came from the humblest of backgrounds, and he met the most unsavory of ends. He was to bring a kingdom, but he died mocked on a Roman cross. Moreover, the basic ideas that the Christians announced were nonsensical. Theirs was a monotheistic religion, yet Christ was the divine son of a god who was also a holy spirit. Educated Romans found it difficult to equate three gods with monotheism.

However, as the sense of being uprooted in a world turned irrational deepened, it was this very absurdity, to use Tertullian's term, which made Christianity convincing. It now appeared to espouse a truth that surpassed mere human understanding. Since the fact that humans had

not given themselves much credit for understanding since the Hellenistic age revealed the mismatch between inherited social cognitive maps
and the environment, the argument that Christianity made no logical
sense seemed actually to intensify its appeal. If scientific reason could
not explain an arrow's flight and political persuasion could not unite
either Greece or Rome, how much credit did human reason deserve?
Faith, a moral commitment that defied logic, now surpassed wisdom
in prestige, and more and more educated, privileged upper-class people
came to believe Jerusalem had surpassed Athens.

By the third century AD not even peace and prosperity were strong
arguments for supporting the earthly city. Disease, economic de-
pression, rising taxes, and political instability reduced the emotional
appeal of Rome. When Diocletian tried to arrest the rot by force, he
only accelerated the pace at which people exiled themselves. Now
economic demands and military dangers added a physical factor to
spiritual flight. St. Augustine was saying what everyone knew when he
announced that Rome was not eternal. He became increasingly
convincing when he argued that people had better look to the salvation
of their eternal souls in the heavenly city. Committing themselves to a
religious vision completely independent of time and space, people were
decoupling themselves from Rome with ever greater totality.

Implementing the Jewish ethic in a less Spartan form, which St. Paul
was able to make even more casual, Christ had urged a revolution upon
humanity. Proclaiming the power of love and brotherhood, he gave
people the promise of a world in which each could trust his neighbor.
To accomplish that revolution, to bring God back in triumph upon the
rainbow, each person had to look into his or her own heart. Purging it
of greed, selfishness, violence, and lust, each person individually would
save his or her own self. When all selves were pure, Jesus would return
and the Kingdom of God would be at hand—not as a secular state but
as an ever-lasting spiritual community.

The Medieval Cognitive Map

Invading barbarians must have delayed the transmutation of human
nature, for even centuries after Christ's resurrection the Second Coming
was yet to occur. But Christianity had not failed. It had planted a
seed that would flower in the European Middle Ages and give rise to
a new type of civilization. Of course, that had not been its intention.
By contrast, the original, essentially communistic teachings of Christ

became institutionalized in a Church that saw itself as heir to Roman grandeur. It took almost 500 years to lay the foundations of the Christian state, but in the eighth century an alliance was forged that was to preserve Europe's independence from the Middle Eastern world by creating an empire like that of Sumer or Rome. Isolated on the periphery of civilization, the people of Europe began teaching themselves a new map and in doing so laid the foundations for a new type of society.

The popes joined forces with the Carolingians to domesticate Europe, while keeping it free from either Muslim or Orthodox interference. When Charlemagne was crowned Holy Roman Emperor, it looked as if the plan was well on its way to success. But two problems immediately presented themselves, and Europe found those problems impossible to solve using conventional techniques. The first was the problem of organizing a defense. The pope needed military force to remain independent of Constantinople, and the Franks needed an army to stop the Muslim advance. But neither had the money to pay for the soldiers, especially since Charles Martel had shown that mounted, armored warrior knights were the only military technology with a chance of success. Knights were dreadfully expensive, and land was the only source of wealth. Organizing a defense based on land meant that to save Europe it was necessary to fragment it.

It was easy to allocate each knight a parcel of land large enough to supply the horses, food, and labor necessary to equip him. But once a knight was ensconced behind a wall on his own land, he was essentially independent. He might owe moral obligation to his feudal lord, but the lord had no way to transport his land-based power and bring it to bear on the knight. Once in possession of the land needed to ensure that the knight could fight barbarians and Arabs, he could no longer be dependably controlled. He might obey a call to arms by baron, count, or king. But if the knight declined service, on his fief and behind his wall he was impregnable.

Knights could use promises of their support to play the major contenders for societal dominance off against each other, which was the second reason Europe failed to organize as a traditional civilizational state. In Rome, the pope wanted to be a god–king, and knights could always justify supporting his cause religiously. That is, whenever an emperor tried to extract the full measure of feudal obligations from his knights, they could find religion at the papal court and rebel against feudal authority. But in Germany, the emperor wanted to be a king–god, and other knights could rally to his side out of feudal obligation or to circumvent religious interference in their secular affairs. Whenever a meddlesome cleric sought to inhibit knightly bloodlusts, knights could always yield to the pull of honor and obey their secular prince. The point is that, playing emperor and pope against each other, the knights shifted sides whenever it seemed that either was strong enough to dominate. The ensuing civil war kept Europe in turmoil even after the barbarians were suppressed, the Vikings were settled, and the Arabs were contained. The balance of power, however, permitted new centers of authority to gather strength.

Of course, the two contenders for control waged a propaganda war against each other, and neither popes nor emperors were above resorting to the most scurrilous charges and deceits. But in the educated clergy, the church had a distinct advantage, and, in the eleventh century, churchmen began to articulate a vision of European society that would eventually produce a cognitive map different from any previously seen. But churchmen were in the unenviable position of trying to bring some order out of chaos using purely verbal arguments. That meant they had to stick fairly close to the facts of experience, at least in the beginning.

It was during the eleventh century that churchmen began to describe medieval Europe as the "society of the three orders." The idea caught on quickly, for a clear class-distinction had developed during the turbulent period following Rome's collapse. The most important job had seemed to be religious, since it was into religion that people poured all their pent-up frustrations resulting from Roman governmental methods. When people no longer felt an allegiance to the earthly city, their only hope of identity was in the heavenly one. So Europe had worked desperately to preserve a group of men "who prayed." This was the first order.

Physical survival was similarly pressing, despite rumors that Christians eager for heavenly rewards offered their bared breasts to invaders. The knights who accepted the obligation to defend localities constituted the second "order" in the emerging medieval society, "those who fight." But fighters and prayers needed food, housing, equipment, and various buildings. They were too specialized actually to support all these activities directly, although the Cistercian monks made many contributions to rebuilding Europe. But a third "order" was available, "those who work," and it was to these enserfed farmers and craftsmen that Europe turned for material necessities.

The symbolic description of European society, once articulated, developed with increasing speed and precision. By the twelfth century, a revival of learning began reintroducing clerics to classical thought, especially to the works of Aristotle. One of Aristotle's major themes, borrowed from Plato, was the idea that the universe was an inter-connected hierarchical structure, a "Great Chain of Being." St. Thomas Aquinas, a Dominican monk of unequaled intelligence and learning, borrowed this conceptualization to refine the vision of a society of the three orders.

It was an apt choice, for everywhere classes of men were bound together in ladders of status and power. The pope was served by his archbishops, bishops, abbots, monks and priests. Kings depended on their counts, earls, barons, and knights. And both clerics and soldiers depended upon merchants, artisans, and serfs. Thus, Aquinas could argue that the universe began in God, pure spirit or intelligence, worked its way downward through the ranks of archangels and angels, passed through humankind, reached into the ranks of animals and plants, and ended in dead matter and the Devil. Each link on the Chain was distinct, but its unique identity depended upon the attributes of the links above and below it. Worms, for instance, were crawling matter, created by mixing the attributes of animals with dead matter. Human beings, who occupied the central link between heaven and earth, were physical creatures with bodies like animals and divine entities with souls like angels.

Of course, it followed from Aquinas's perspective that the pope should be dominant over the emperor, for spirit prevailed over matter. The Church officially embraced this idea in the doctrine of the "two swords." Moreover, in the organic quality of the Aquinian vision, most Europeans saw their world mapped realistically. A chain is only as strong as its weakest link, and the chain as a whole must take priority over any individual link. In the doctrine of the "just price," medieval economics practiced this idea. The price of any good was set by the Church acting for the community. It prevented gorging during poor harvests and bankruptcy during periods of abundance, because the just price fixed value in terms that could preserve the existing order.

Independent of market forces, prices were set in terms of costs plus the profit necessary to maintain the seller in his established position on the Great Chain. A serf could not be overcharged for bread fol-lowing a drought, for example, since he might then starve to death and the community would be deprived of his services during the next agricultural cycle. But saving the soul of the seller was equally important, for inflating prices might make the seller rich and camels had less trouble passing through the eyes of needles than did rich men entering the gates of heaven. Of course, by squelching ambition, the organic society of the three orders kept everyone in his proper hierarchical position and retained social stability despite the vagaries of harvests.

The initial conditions in which medieval society was forged were so unstable that freezing society in the rigid image of an interlocking chain made good sense. Amidst the turbulence of collapse and invasion, no risks could be taken. Every community needed to know that its knight would be in his castle, trained and eager to fight; every Christian needed to know that prayers would be said for his or her salvation; every priest needed to know where his next meal was coming from. There was no margin for error, especially after the Viking attacks began.

The Breakup of the Medieval Cognitive Map

By about AD1000, Europe had stabilized. Trade with the Middle East began to revive; silver was later discovered in central Europe. New crops, plows, and rotations generated agricultural surpluses and a population explosion. The knights who had crusaded in the Holy Land had acquired appetites for the finely manufactured luxuries Europe had not seen for nearly a millennium. Tradesmen sought to exploit those appetites by organizing fairs. Fairs gathered large populations that churches, miracles, and relics could exploit financially. And local princes began looking toward the new futures made possible by taxing trade in money.

But the merchant classes and towns that began to appear after AD1200 had no links on the Great Chain of Being, and social mobility was inexplicable in terms of a map that froze social relationships. The earliest cultural strains reflecting a mismatch between map and territory appeared, reasonably enough, in the few parts of Europe—such as southern France—where urbanization, prosperity, and commerce had flourished first. But the agents of the earthly shifts stirring beneath European feet were usually secular figures with limited learning. They were not equipped to praise the virtues of upward mobility based on material prosperity. Instead, they felt a growing sense of guilt, for their experience violated the norms and values of the Great Chain.

Naturally, the town-dwelling merchants of southern France expressed their own sense of misgiving by blaming the Church. They quickly passed from condemning clerical corruption to exploring a variety of heresies encountered in the Middle East. Waldensians, Burgomites, Cathars, etc. all gathered members and intensified their followers' sense of alienation. But while these twelfth- and thirteenth-century heresies showed the seams were straining in the society of the three orders, established institutions were still powerful enough to repress them. The Church invented the Inquisition to destroy the Cathars, and the Inquisition was equipped with military might by inducing landless knights like Simon de Montford to unsheathe their swords in the interest of piety—and stability. The resulting bloodbath was so noxious that even some of the knights are thought to have protested. But the Church prevailed.

Challenges from inside were also effectively dealt with. Northern Italy revived soon after southern France, and its spiritual strains produced behaviors like that of Francis of Assisi. Rejecting the inherited wealth that might have jeopardized salvation, Francis embraced a religion of love and communal poverty that embarrassed Church authorities. Instead of destroying him, however, the Church domesticated the threat by letting the Franciscans organize a monastic order under papal control. It was a decision the popes later regretted, for by the fourteenth century Franciscan monks were among the most vociferous and ingenious critics of the official Church.

The papal ploy would probably have been more immediately effective had not the King of France grown angry at the Church's ability to tax commerce in France and siphon it into Roman coffers. King Philip IV needed that money, for it was only with money that he could overcome the fragmenting propensities of feudalism. Money was portable. It could be collected everywhere throughout the kingdom, transported to Paris, and there used to pay mercenary soldiers who would travel to any province and destroy the castles of recalcitrant knights. The destruction was more certain once gunpowder came into circulation, but cannons cost even more than soldiers. Every tithe that went to Rome, therefore, was a sapping of royal strength permitting the continuance of feudal decentralization.

Knights may have been the original markets for reviving European trade, but, by the fourteenth century, the explosive, violence-prone behaviors that had once secured survival from marauding bands of Vikings had become an obstacle to economic progress. Local knights demanded taxes, charged tariffs, abided by their own laws, and frequently broke out into feudal warfare—even in the marketplaces where the fairs were held. Knights, in other words, inhibited commerce and were bad for business. So kings had natural allies in the rising middle classes, for if a centralized authority could be created, internal tariffs would disappear, only one tax would have to be paid, a single market would be created, just one set of laws would obtain throughout, and the internal violence that made business unpredictable would be repressed.

Businessmen would pay taxes to kings, provided kings supported their economic and social ambitions. Both were to the kings' advantage. Not only would establishing a stable market increase royal revenues; absorbing middle-class talents into royal bureaucracies would increase their effectiveness. Of course, any royal office meant that a bourgeois merchant had acquired social status, for the merchant or lawyer on a mission for the king was an "official" person. But moving up the social ladder weakened the organic structure of the Great Chain, which was being threatened by a variety of other forces as well.

Population growth from the mid-thirteenth century onward was necessitating the expansion of European agriculture into frontier areas. Serfs, of course, had little interest either in abandoning what few comforts they had acquired for rough frontier living or for trading the devils they knew for ones they had never met. So knights had to entice serfs into virgin territories. That was done by reducing the serfs' feudal obligations, meaning that even serfs were less trapped by their inherited identities than previously.

Thinking itself clever, the nobility accelerated the process by switching from rents in service and kind to fixed money payments. Money payments let the landlords buy the consumer goods for which they hungered from merchants at fairs. But increased demand sparked a cycle of inflation that, by 1300, left most knights in serious debt and many serfs virtually independent. When the Black Death struck in 1348, it devastated a medieval social structure that was already coming apart. By that point, the popes were already living in Babylonian exile in Avignon, having been reduced to employees of the French king. Towns and merchants had sprung up everywhere. Knights were no longer independent, and the emperor was as threatened by the emerging nationalism as the pope. Clearly, the Great Chain of Being no longer matched the European territory.

But no other image was available to make sense of experience. The plight of European intellectuals was made clear in the fifteenth century by both Nicholas of Cusa, a cardinal, and Pico della Mirandola, one of the first secular intellectuals. Nicholas of Cusa worked out the logical implications of the medieval cognitive map and found they contradicted themselves with a Gödelian viciousness. If God were the creator and had infinite power, for instance, He ought to have made an infinite universe. But an infinite universe could not be mapped by the Great Chain. It would, to begin with, have the very sort of infinite regress whose logical impossibility St. Thomas had used to prove the existence of God. Similarly, Pico saw a world in which every day witnessed paupers becoming bankers, great families sinking into poverty, and everything in constant flux. He tried to extract a measure of hope from this pessimistic view by arguing that humankind was born at the center of the Great Chain but not locked into place. Rather, each of us was free to rise or fall according to individual abilities. We could rise to the very ranks of angels. But we could also, as so many Renaissance people so obviously did, sink into diabolical pits of sin and corruption.

This world of pure, rampant individuality was, like the Hellenistic age, an anarchy that could not be mapped. Consequently, neither could its future be predicted. Fortuna, the goddess of chance, was ultimately in charge, and no man's wit was powerful enough to control his destiny. People are, said Rabelais, more animal than human, and our greatest virtue is the ability to laugh—a virtue exercisable only behind the walls of an Epicurean garden. Agrippa was more cynical, arguing that "man is to man a wolf," and that whatever laws of nature there were got honored most regularly in the breach. Montaigne counseled that we withdraw, practice stoic virtues, and talk to our cats.

But while a world in cultural chaos distressed the sensitive, the more adventurous spirits set out to explore the possibilities of a wide-open social situation. Their guide was Machiavelli, who justified any means to achieve self-selected ends. Machiavelli's own examples, however, were, like Cesare Borgia, notable failures, and it is unlikely that Machiavelli himself aspired to an amoral world. Rather, as his many volumes on civil virtue in antiquity suggest, he was only willing to use ruthless means to build a new society in which people would again be moral. He rightly excused the "prince" from any inherited medieval moral restrictions during the creative phase of social reconstruction, since in the absence of a coherent society there was no foundation for morals, and in the absence of an accepted cognitive map no way to allocate virtue. But he dreamed of a united Italy in which citizens would demonstrate their commitment to public good over private advantage by, for instance, eager service in a volunteer army. He put his eggs in the wrong basket.

Machiavelli believed society could be reorganized from the top down. While it is possible to operate societies top-down, as traditional civilizations did, societies generate themselves bottom-up. Medieval society, inspired by a carpenter and amplified by slaves, is the best historical example. But where were the people able to generate a coherent society to come from? The answer to that rhetorical question proves how unrealistic it is to try to control social evolution, or even to guide it. The people out of whom a new European society self-organized in the modern era were produced by the most backward-looking, self-consciously obstructionist personalities in sixteenth-century Europe: the fundamentalist leaders of the Protestant Reformation.

After Luther, Protestant clerics had shattered the Catholic Church's last vestiges of universal authority by denying the pope's power to control entrance through the Pearly Gates and the Church's role in directing behavior from the outside in. In Luther's theology, which expresses the bankruptcy of the medieval cognitive map by demonstrating that no rational path to understanding is possible, people would not be saved by "Good Works," the traditional Catholic theology. In the absence of a societal cognitive map, they did not know what was good, had no idea how to achieve it, and were too confused to choose good over evil. But, as Luther discovered in a blinding flash of inspiration, people could be saved through "Faith Alone." That was not supposed to be a license to immorality. Rather, Luther wanted "every man to be a monk his whole life through." Luther took the individual who had fallen through the tattered fabric of medieval culture and stood him on his own two feet again.

Calvin's contribution was even more extreme. Believing that people were too corrupt ever to control themselves or earn salvation, Calvin decided that this was predetermined by a divine fiat over which we had no control. Again, ruthlessly paring away the whole structure of medieval community that had safely nestled humanity, Calvin placed individual people alone and naked before the judgmental eye of an infinite and angry God. While this description of human experience reflects the alienation of social collapse, Calvin's other doctrines offered a way, in Erich Fromm's (1947) phrase, to "escape from freedom." In particular, Calvin taught that those few humans chosen by God for salvation would be the agents through which His will operated in the world. Since, by definition, God could not fail, those of us who prospered could expect to see worldly success as an outward sign of spiritual election. It does not take a Freudian psychologist to suppose that devout Calvinists would repress doubts about salvation by working hard to make money and living frugally to accumulate it.

But inwardly motivated people stimulated to work hard were a new component of societies. Civilized states had previously extracted more work from the majority of their subjects than nomadic groups had, but civilized societies extracted work by what Herbert Spencer called "coercive cooperation." Calvinism did on a grand scale what only the Cistercian monks had previously accomplished on a small one— Calvinism motivated people throughout the ranks of secular society to work for themselves. But this dramatic change in human behavior was not entirely spiritual in origin. There were economic factors involved as well, the most important of which was the emergence of private property.

Like Protestantism, private property isolated people individually. A man on his own estate stood alone beyond the bounds of society. He could do whatever he chose, and no one had the right to invade his land and object. But while private property gave individual rights a material foundation, independence from the community also meant that the individual incurred private responsibilities. If he managed his land carefully and husbanded its resources well, a man could expect "to live off his own" quite comfortably. But should he be lazy, stupid, reckless, or rash, no one else was obliged to keep him. Private property meant that no one was anybody else's brother anymore.

Religious and economic individuality introduced the prospect of social anarchy, as sixteenth- and seventeenth-century conservatives repeatedly pointed out. Everyone was more-or-less free of inherited masters, but there was no way to communicate information from one person to another. People were so desperate that they had abandoned a society that could not solve problems for them and developed techniques for solving problems individually. In the great Renaissance figures, like Urbino or Leonardo, these highly individualized personalities took great pride in their uniqueness. One of them, the goldsmith Benvenuto Cellini, even invented autobiography so that everyone else could appreciate just how fascinating his self-created identity was. But a world of mercenaries, confidence men, and cutthroats is not a society, nor is a world polarized by religious sectarianism. Some way had to be found to transcend religious differences and to map a world of competing individualists.

The religious movements that had done so much to destroy medieval society and lay the psychological foundations for a modern one made the reunification of society almost impossible. Intense commitments to the various forms of Christianity turned people against one another with a vindictiveness that exceeded Machiavelli's most bloody examples by several orders of magnitude. The first country to suffer was France. There, the Reformation made little initial progress, despite the fact that many leading intellectuals and pious Christians shared Luther's basic ideas. But Luther had succeeded because his religious visions happened to coincide with the political aspirations of his local prince, Frederick the Wise. Aspiring to be independent of both the pope and the emperor, Frederick—like princes throughout the Germanic center of Europe—had rallied to the Protestants' cause. The eventual settlement, after decades of warfare and rebellion, was that every prince decided the religion of his region. In other words, Lutheranism helped create state churches throughout much of central and northern Europe.

But France had enjoyed the benefits of formal independence from papal power since the Pragmatic Sanction of Bourges was signed in 1438. No matter how compelling the theological arguments, therefore, French kings saw no advantage to rocking their political boat by engaging in religious polemic. Since Lutherans believed that the prince determined the religion of his domain, in France his followers had no alternative to obeying their Catholic king.

Calvin's more radical disciples had other ideas. They argued that social and political leaders, the magistrates, had a moral obligation to destroy a king whose false religion endangered the salvation of their subjects. They called it *tyrannicide*. How predestined salvation could be jeopardized by royal whimsy was never explained, but in the writings of several politically determined Calvinists it became the basis for the first justification of revolution in the West. The result was a decades-long civil war punctuated by some of the most ruthless savagery in European history.

Eventually, the first coolly modern heads prevailed in the writings of Jean Bodin and the *politiques*. Arguing that it made no difference whether France was Catholic or Protestant if all Frenchmen were dead, they concluded that national survival was more important than spiritual integrity. Their leader, the first Bourbon king, Henri IV, summed up the whole idea when he abandoned his Protestant faith to become king of a mostly Catholic France. "Paris," he said, "is worth a Mass." He issued the Edict of Nantes in 1598, guaranteeing to Huguenots, as French Protestants were called, the legal right to practice their own faith in their own churches free of interference from either Catholic vigilantes or the state. Religion was now a private matter of little interest to the state.

In England things were equally tumultuous. Henry VIII had embraced a kind of Lutheranism, although he was officially "Protector of the Faith" for having written a pamphlet denouncing Luther. But Henry believed that a divorce from his Spanish queen was essential to the preservation of his dynasty, and a pope dominated by her uncle was unable to supply it. Henry won instant approval for repudiating Catholicism at home by breaking up the vast monastic lands and distributing them to bourgeois and lesser gentry who served him loyally and well. His daughter Elizabeth rode the tiger of religious dissension by studiously ignoring it, at least in public. "Open no windows into men's souls," she advised her minister Burghley. But when the Stuarts inherited the throne of England, the slide into anarchy was greased. James I managed to survive growing religious tensions by concealing his own beliefs. His son, Charles I, took the idea of the Divine Right of Monarchs so seriously that, simple-mindedly, he tried to ignore Parliament and smuggle Catholicism back into Britain. The civil war that followed led to his execution and the first successful revolution in European history. It was, more than the Renaissance, the point at which "Modern" society self-organized.

The Rise of the Cognitive Map of Modern Science

The process of cultural change in Europe can be tracked with special clarity by comparing the writings of Thomas Hobbes and John Locke, the two most prominent seventeenth-century English philosophers. Like other political philosophers, their whole arguments depended essentially on the definitions of human nature with which they began. But a definition of human nature is always a commentary on, or a "mapping" of, the people around the philosopher. Even though they appear to be writing in purely abstract theoretical terms, Hobbes and Locke were describing their world in their political analyses.

Writing during the bloodiest phases of the English Civil War, Hobbes described human nature as ruthlessly appetitive, cunning, and unrestrained. Every one of us, he thought, wants the same things, is equally capable of getting what he wants, and is uninhibited by any internal conscience or sense of limits. Since we all want the same apples, we fight with one another constantly in a "war of all against all." Life, therefore, is "nasty, cold, mean, brutish, and short." The only hope of survival lies in the erection of a Leviathan state, whose absolute power stands like the hangman beside every human being. The fear that certain death immediately follows any transgression alone inhibits human avarice and makes society possible.

Writing after the Civil War had been over for a generation, Locke postulated a human nature that was inherently rational and capable of learning from experience. Thus, if people are bad it is not because they have to be bad, but because society has taught them to be. In the absence of society, of course, people would still want apples. In fact, Locke offered the first moral defense of private property by claiming that we have a natural right to anything with which we mix our own labor. Thus if I pick some apples they are rightly mine, not anybody else's.

But what happens when someone else comes along who wants my apples? Locke admitted a Hobbesean response was possible. The apple-less person might attack, trying to steal what is mine by natural right. But that was a risky business, Locke said, and hardly worth the trouble when barter is so easy and so much safer. To be sure, one trader might not offer what the other feels is fair, but that does not mean that war necessarily results. On the contrary, since war is threatening to both parties, it is likely that rational men would turn to some neutral referee to arbitrate. In other words, Locke did not see human nature as loving, caring, and eager to share: in the state of nature there were likely to be disputes. But Locke did not believe "the howling of jackals" would frighten humanity into "the jaws of lions." People would not erect the Leviathan state and surrender all rights to it just to survive. That was unnecessary, for the people Locke was describing in his theory of human nature had learned—through Protestantism and the responsi-bilities of private property—to govern themselves.

If by Locke's time it was obvious that society had begun to self-organize in a new form that depended on inner-directedness and that respected individuality, the problem still remained of how that world was to be mapped collectively. But great steps forward had been taken, despite, if not because of, the confusion. In a simple sense, what was needed was a way to bridge the gap between polarized religious con-victions. Equally, some way had to be found to view the world that private initiative had vastly expanded but that transcended inherited moral and spiritual issues. When people confronted one another over their heart-felt beliefs, there was little hope of joining them together if their hearts could be filled with different beliefs—especially since each person was responsible only for his or her self.

The passionate intensity with which even the most intelligent people interacted during the Renaissance and Reformation measured the des-peration they felt in living in a world that inherited beliefs no longer mapped (Toulmin 1990). Medieval tradition, for instance, held that God governed the world, rewarding the just and punishing the ungodly. The indiscriminate slaughter associated with either the Black Death or the religious wars rendered that faith transparently foolish. The Scholastic philosophers, quoting St. Augustine, had proved the world was flat, but Columbus and Magellan experienced its curvature in their own flesh, as Campanella pointed out. Obviously, before any reintegration could take place, the past had to be purged.

Francis Bacon and René Descartes led the campaign to liberate the present through the method of "radical doubt." According to them, nothing was to be taken on faith, no matter what its authority. Everything was to be examined skeptically and "put to the test." This would probably have amounted to little more than yet another philosophical argument, as it had in Greece, had not an Italian mathematician and engineer, Galileo Galilei, stumbled upon the telescope. The telescope, which had been invented as a toy and which Galileo sold as a maritime device, was turned by him on the heavens. There it proved remarkably suited for resolving disputes by the discovery of incontestable, "value-free" facts.

The most important test case was the dispute over the heliocentric universe. Copernicus had argued that the planets' motion around the sun means that Venus passes through phases. Near the earth it would appear large but only partially illuminated, while at its farthest distance from earth Venus would appear small but be fully illuminated. As these ideas were rejected by disciples of Aristotle and most religious authorities, a hot debate ensued. But while Copernicus's prediction puts his thesis in the category of scientific theory, the naked eye could not detect changes in either the apparent shape or size of distant Venus. So, as with religion, all people could do was to argue about what they believed.

Galileo's telescope brought Venus closer and made it larger. When telescopic observations showed that the planet passed through the predicted phases, Galileo took it as proof that the Copernican system was as real as Copernicus thought. But more importantly, the telescope brought in an apparently neutral observer. It was neither an Aristotelian nor a Copernican, neither a Catholic nor a Protestant. Having no mind, the telescope had no philosophy; having no heart, it had no emotionally excited beliefs. Here, then, was a method—instrumental observation—that could bridge the gap between human minds.

Galileo followed up this discovery of the scientific method with a series of brilliant experiments in which he demonstrated relative motion, the flaw in Aristotle's theory of motion, and the law of falling bodies. In all these cases, he began the positive work of building on the ground cleared by skeptical doubt. But to bridge the gap between passionate beliefs, Galileo had to introduce a radical set of presuppositions. Basic to Galileo's philosophy was the idea that the world exists external to and independent of the people observing it. We can stand outside nature and, provided we depend upon unbiased instruments, can reconstruct it accurately in our minds.

The problem, Galileo thought, is that people had traditionally relied only upon their minds to construct an image of the world. But those images were always distorted because the human mind contains "secondary characteristics" like color and taste, values and morals. There is nothing wrong with that, of course; it is simply the way the mind is. But when we take our inner experience as a guide to external reality we get a faulty picture. In our minds, the secondary characteristics like color and taste, values and morals, represent the world. But sweetness, said Galileo, depends entirely on taste buds, odors on nostrils, and judgments on prejudices. These things do not exist in the real world: there only matter and motion exist. Matter and motion, which are describable quantitatively because they can be counted, weighed, and measured, represent the "primary characteristics" of the real world.

Of course, it is precisely over whether an object is blue or green, sweet or bitter, good or evil that people contend. If they concern themselves exclusively with these things, they can never reach agreement, and "the great organ of our philosophy," said Galileo, must remain forever "discordant." But if people learn to focus on what instrumental measures tell them about the world, then they get an undistorted picture about which they need not argue. To be sure, one scientist may report that a body of a certain mass and shape fell at a certain rate, while another may give entirely different results. But there are no grounds for argument here. It does not matter if we think the one rate is moral and the other immoral, the one body Protestant and the other Catholic. We need only to repeat the experiment and check the arithmetic. As Leibniz was soon to say, to resolve a scientific disagreement all we need to do is say "let us calculate."

A picture of the world from which all secondary, qualitative characteristics had been cut out was so abstract that it could be applied universally, as Newton soon showed. But, as with any other new idea, this one could only be amplified by public endorsement after its utility had been demonstrated. Interestingly enough, the message that emerged for the public was significantly different from what Newton had in mind privately.

Newton captured the public imagination, under pressure from

Halley, in the *Philosophiae Naturalis Principia Mathematica* of 1687. Chapter 2 of the *Principia* demonstrated with geometrical certainty and experimental clarity that planets did rotate around the sun in orbits described by Kepler's three laws. Newton himself did not believe, however, that geometrical descriptions explained in reference to matter and force were complete. A hermetic magus and religious mystic, he was sure that God played an active role in nature, which only mystical numerology could ferret out. But he had not had time to include all the relevant arguments in the *Principia.* That book was written under the threat of Hooke's claim to have already solved the riddle of the universe.

Following publication of the *Principia*, Newton suffered a nervous breakdown. For nearly two years he did no work and seems to have understood very little of what went on around him. With recovery, he began editing the *Principia*, intending to supplement it with lengthy discussions of his religious, numerological, and alchemic doctrines. But as the revised edition neared completion, Newton suddenly realized that he was famous throughout the Western world, for he was the genius who had explained the whole creation without reference to God, alchemy, or numerology. Newton was the personification of human genius at its pinnacle—"God said, 'Let Newton be' | And all was light," according to Alexander Pope. He now faced an agonizing choice: should he let his book stand as published and reap unequaled praise, or should he set the record straight and announce to the Republic of Letters that this is not what he meant after all? Newton chose the former course, while keeping a scout's eye out for opportunities to advance his true beliefs.

But the time for mysticism had passed. Newton's *Principia* was the nucleation that permitted the European cognitive map to evolve. It is easy to see why Newton's ideas successfully blossomed into a new-style cognitive map, but harder to understand how that cognitive map actually worked and what it accomplished. There were three reasons for Newton's success.

First and foremost, his ideas provided precisely the sort of "clear and certain" knowledge people had been looking for since the Black Death. Newton's principles were absolute. Deterministic and universal, they required that every particle in every corner of the universe behave exactly as the laws of motion indicated, yesterday, today, and tomorrow. Moreover, although some period of lingering uncertainty might be necessary while complete knowledge is being accumulated, the inevitability of a God's-eye view of the whole world had been established. To be sure, not everything had been discovered: some things remained unknown even about the Newtonian system itself. Newton, for instance, did not know what gravity is. But he knew how to measure it now, and he could guarantee that following the Galilean method would ultimately resolve the definitional conundrum. Finally, when the method was followed systematically, and "crucial experiments" were carried out, the scientist had indisputable knowledge of the world. The modern cognitive map written in the language of science took the powers and characteristics the Middle Ages had attributed to God, and bestowed them on Nature.

Secondly, Newton's ideas were publicly endorsed because modern Europeans could recognize their own experiences in the model he articulated. He postulated a world made up of "corpuscles," atomized units of matter whose every action was quantifiable. Now individualized competitors operating in a market economy where reality was measured in money must have looked very much like Newton's descriptions of nature, even to themselves. Similarly, Newton's *Principia* was written at the time the "Bloodless Revolution" finally and definitively established a "Balanced Polity." Henceforth, in Britain, free men governed themselves according to law. Newton's *Principia* mapped nature in the constitutional terms with which a generation of civil strife had made a significant part of the British middle class all too familiar. They must have seen a solar system that governed itself because of the rational laws its bodies obeyed as promise and reward for their efforts.

The third reason for Newton's success was that his ideas appeared useful to the nation states that had emerged as successors to traditional societies. Charles II, the restored king of Britain, quickly realized that astronomical knowledge improved the navigational skills of both his merchant and his military fleets. Thanks to Newton, the heavens could be plotted and the future positions of the heavenly bodies predicted. British ships could henceforth sail to every corner of the Earth faster and more directly than their Dutch and French competitors. Of course, Galilean studies of motion, which Newton perfected, also made artillery fire more precise. Since wealth and power flowed from science, Charles II founded the Royal Society for the Advancement of Learning, and Continental monarchs quickly opened similar institutions of their own.

The consequences of Newton's new social cognitive map were both dramatic and rapid. A pessimistic culture seeking to escape from freedom now became an optimistic culture bent on expanding freedom, at least for its own people and institutions. Europeans felt confident that they possessed the key to unlocking the mysteries of nature, for seeing behind the "bloomin', buzzin' confusion" of experience. As Fontenelle put it around 1700, the world appeared like the face of a clock. For millennia, ignorant and opinionated people had marveled at the movement of the clock's hands and made up stories to explain the apparent miracle. Thanks to Newton, Europeans acquired the capacity to look behind the face, to see the gears and pulleys at work, and to comprehend the mechanism underlying the surface appearances.

Inspired by Voltaire, scores of intellectuals, called *philosophes*, embarked upon the great adventure of bringing light to the world and of mapping its most hidden recesses. They railed against religious intolerance in the name of Nature's God, which was equally revealed to all peoples everywhere and never capriciously broke its own laws. They demanded, with Cesare Beccaria, the ending of judicial torture and the development of rational legal codes in which private rights were respected and "cruel and unusual punishments" were forbidden. With the wit and clarity of Diderot, they proclaimed the dawn of a "natural morality" in which humanity would finally be released from the artificial restraints of superstition and tradition. In Scotland, Adam Smith, the Newton of economics, discovered the social equivalent of laws of motion—the laws of supply and demand—and demonstrated how by arranging economies naturally the wealth of nations could increase.

The Enlightenment heirs to Newton thought that they knew how the world was constituted, what controlled its actions, and how to organize society in a scientific way. They were ushering in a new age in which, for literally the first time, human beings could be happy. All that was necessary was for human beings to approach society with the same attitude Newton had approached nature, discover its basic laws, and bring to earth the harmonies that stabilized the solar system. But that was not so easy: the Reformation and the spreading of private property created individuals who obeyed only their own inner directions. How was their behavior to be correlated so that a coherent society could self-organize?

Using modern science to organize societies proved more difficult than expected. On the one hand, it was possible to use scientific research to learn more about nature and apply that knowledge technologically. There are hints in the modifications of the steam engine by Watt that science was indeed being used to access more energy and process more matter as early as the eighteenth century. But real "progress" did not come until the advent of the German dye industry and the various electrochemical technologies of the later nineteenth century. It is reasonable to maintain that these developments contributed to improving the material foundations of civilized life in the West. Certainly, applications of medical technology in the twentieth century have prolonged life. So in these areas, science seemed to be delivering on the Baconian promise to build an earthly utopia by harnessing the forces of nature to meet human needs. Arming itself with "Modern Western Science," European society began to out-compete its tradition-bound neighbors.

Though there were advances on the material side of the ledger, problems on the spiritual side rose quickly. The fundamental distinction between how people were thinking—qualitatively—and how nature was supposed to act—quantitatively—made the transfer of science to social and political sectors almost impossible. Qualitative thought involved subjective judgments about values and ideas. But scientific descriptions denied the objective reality of judgments, values, and ideas. Modern thinkers found themselves in the odd position of trying to reconstruct human society with a cognitive map from which, in Erwin Schrödinger's words, "the human personality had been quite cut out."

The major drawback from which modern science suffered as a societal cognitive map was that, despite its skill in describing the world, modern science was silent when called upon to prescribe action. Behavior is triggered or inhibited by value symbols, which "enframe" the actor (Goffman 1973). Ancient and medieval societies could enframe their relationships and institutions by appealing to God. But in a universe reduced to matter and motion, which was everywhere "conformable to itself," there was no external authority to enframe relationships or institutions. Erstwhile legislators, said Rousseau, had thus to "be as gods." They had to rise above the fray, envisage an idealized future, wrap it in the cloak of its own necessity, and do what was good for the world whether the world knew it or not (Camus 1956).

The first indications of how problematical it was going to be to reform society on the basis of a cognitive map "that cared no more for good over evil than for heat over cold" appeared during the French Revolution. Leaders like Robespierre and Saint-Just were convinced by the Age of Reason that human happiness was attainable in time and in history. But they ruled a country ravaged by poverty and torn by civil war. They found to their chagrin that force was needed to solve multiple crises simultaneously. But how could force be justified? The Committee of Public Safety could not appeal to any external authority—there was no God from whom they could receive The Law by climbing a mountain. They had to find in the cauldron of political action the justification for political action. If people had to be killed, it could only be for the good of the People. The self-referentiality of the societal feedback loop became visible for the first time, and it launched generations of European intellectuals on a desperate ideological search for morally binding values. If society was, like everything else in nature, simply a mechanism, then clear and certain moral knowledge should be attainable. Moreover, if there were laws of motion that controlled the trajectories of people, then the future of society should be as transparent as the future of the solar system. The great "Laplacean Illusion" was as seductive in politics as it was in physics.

But the political ideologue had to be "scientific," he had to stand outside the political system, observe it objectively, and calculate its future. In the name of humanity, the ideologue had to dehumanize himself. Experience taught, from 1789 on, that the predicted future was not always fast in coming. Delay, however, meant that human lives were being wasted, broken by poverty, and crushed by superstition. In the absence of a Heavenly City, each wasted life was an insult to the whole of nature. These offenses to the smooth fulfillment of human destiny, enlightened thinkers concluded, were obviously the result of subjective values perverting the behavior of a handful of sick minds. Reformers, therefore, had to emulate Robespierre and Saint-Just. Ensuring first that their own hearts were pure, they had then to steel themselves to perform the revolutionary surgery history demanded by cutting away the people who stood in the way of progress.

Chernyshevsky in Russia was among the first to articulate the vision of the modern reformer as the self-appointed, self-disciplined hero who did the dirty work necessary to save the world. But his fictional hero, Rakhmetov, was merely a mapping of underworld figures like Babeuf, Buonarroti, Blanqui, Bakunin, Marx, and Engels. These were genuinely tragic figures, dedicated to a cause for which they sacrificed everything but which corrupted them as surely as a life of crime would have. They were the victims of the modern cognitive map, repressing their humanity because nature, they thought, is only a machine. Awed by the accomplishments of technology that transformed the world beneath their feet, they were convinced science was the royal road to Truth. Convinced that underlying laws permitted the future to be logically deduced, they were nevertheless inflamed by a passionate desire to accomplish the historical mission before more lives were lost to selfishness and ignorance.

The nineteenth and early twentieth centuries were riddled with revolutions, almost all of which failed. Some, like the Bolshevik, managed to gain power for their initiators, but their consequences seem, if anything, even more ineffective. The problem is not merely the psychological agony of trying to justify the deeds of the people in the name of the People by constantly escalating the violence used to achieve the noble end of abolishing violence. The problem is also the choice of the strategy to bring about societal self-organization.

Another strategy was developed in the newly founded United States, where a constitution of a new type was written in 1787. Traditionally, constitutions were defined as the formal arrangement of the parts of a society, comparable to the parts of a biological body. Eighteenth-century theorists meant by "constitution" the fixed organization of a society inherited from its ancestors. How a society was "constituted," in other words, was determined by nature and by historical experience.

Most revolutionaries were "blue-print" thinkers (Popper 1962). They were convinced that scientific analysis could not only demonstrate that previous societies were unjustly constituted, but could also display the architecture for how future societies ought to be arranged. When the fifty-five Founding Fathers of the American republic gathered in Philadelphia, they intended to create a nation in that traditional sense, to determine what arrangement of classes, territories, and subsystems was right and proper. Most of them, like their European contemporaries, had a clear idea of what the internal relations defining society should be. The problem immediately became, however, that few of the delegates shared one another's visions. Big states wanted to dominate small ones, seaboard states to dominate frontier areas, slave states to dominate free ones—and vice versa.

The delegates could have argued interminably, as each of them sought coalitions to achieve their goals. But the foundling nation was perilously perched on the edge of collapse—bankrupt and torn by dissent, with the British lion lurking off-shore, eager to pounce—and extended argument would simply have meant political failure. The delegates therefore abandoned their attempt to shape the nation and decided instead to seek agreement about the rules by which the nation would, over time and through experience, shape itself. They decoupled the politico-legal structure from the culture (Berthoff and Murrin 1973). The U.S. Constitution broke symmetry with previous social systems because it did not establish the rules by which parties, factions, and sections shall be arranged once and for all. It did not, in the traditional sense, "constitute" a society by formalizing the relationships between parts of the body politic. Instead, the U.S. Constitution established the rules of procedure, the rules for making rules, by which the nation is to arrange itself over time and through experience.

The Constitution introduced the possibility that a society can represent itself in a new way. It does not describe what the society is but how the society works. By emphasizing rules for the making of rules, it does not commit the United States to any particular policy. As a result, the structure of American society can adjust to a variety of environmental situations. As collective action transforms the environment, increasing the flows of information, energy, and matter, the society can alter its internal relationships. Of course, to preserve stability amidst change, it is necessary for all participants to accept the rules for making rules, the rules of the game. But since these rules do not commit the society to any particular arrangement, it is in the best interest of all concerned to follow them.

There are collective benefits to be had from this kind of structural flexibility. One of the most obvious is the vast amounts of wealth that a society of freely acting, politically empowered individuals can generate. Each individual, privately rewarded for his or her own initiative, is encouraged to search out opportunities, even opportunities that may destabilize existing formal arrangements. The ability to locate and exploit wealth on a previously unequaled scale is, no doubt, the major key—and the indisputable proof—of modern Western society's evolutionary transformation of traditional civilization. Valuing knowledge of how things are done rather than what things are done, the West has been extremely adept at locating wealth and multiplying the population of its products.

Whether the West and other societies can continue to adapt to the changes their collective actions precipitate is an issue that we shall examine in the next chapter.

CHAPTER THREE

Current Changes in Cognitive Maps

No creature on earth is as concerned with creating images of the future as is the human. It is our passion and our obsession, and we are good at it. Our brains are uniquely designed for this work.

Of all the structures of the brain, it is the frontal lobe, the most recent evolutionary development of the neocortex, that is uniquely involved in creating images of the future, and with projecting ourselves as active agents into those images. In an exhaustive examination of observations made both in the clinic and in the laboratory, psychologist and systems analyst David Loye (1983) concluded that the frontal lobe acts in a managerial fashion, consulting the rational analytic faculty of the left hemisphere and the intuitive spatial capacities of the right hemisphere to formulate overall agendas for action, and to issue orders for their execution.

Tens of thousands of prefrontal lobotomies were performed on psychiatric patients between the invention of the procedure in the early 1940s and its demise in the 1960s. The operation could be carried out in the physician's office simply by inserting a surgical instrument through the thin bone above the eye socket and sweeping it back and forth laterally through the tissue of the forward-most aspect of the frontal lobe. The patient could return home immediately, exhibiting nothing more visible than a set of black eyes that returned to normal within a few days. Patients showed considerable reductions in anxiety and emotional agitation, and became much easier to manage. Psychiatrists said that no significant damage was done to the patients' abilities, and indeed in more than one investigation demonstrated that they themselves could not tell a lobotomized individual from a normal one! The families of the patients said they had lost their souls.

In his thoughtful review of this material, Loye reveals that a considerable number of abnormalities in fact surfaced in lobotomized individuals. Besides losing interest in other people—a symptom that the psychiatrists took to be an improvement—they seemed to take no interest in the future. The Russian neurologist Alexander Luria observed that frontal lobe damage caused patients to lose the ability to plan for the future:

Although their movements are externally intact, the behavior . . . is grossly disturbed. They have difficulty creating plans, they are unable to choose actions corresponding to these plans, they readily submit to the influence of irrelevant stimuli, and they vary the course of an action once it has been started. (1966: 531)

It is perhaps not surprising that patients who can't think about the future have remarkably low anxiety levels. The capacity to worry seriously, or at least to ponder the future deeply, is one of the unique capacities of the fully functional human mind.

Not surprisingly, anxiety is a common feature of today's world. The fact is that, in the last decade of the twentieth century, we are living in an era of transition, as different from life in the recent past as the grasslands were from the caves, and settled villages from life in nomadic tribes. Living in an era of transition is also an unusual adventure. In the span of a single lifetime, patterns of existence have seldom if ever changed as profoundly and as rapidly as today. But, though the speed of change is exhilarating, the transformations it produces are not without danger. Science and technology have raised human living standards for some millions beyond all expectations, but social inequities, political stresses, and unreflective uses of technology are polarizing the great majority of humanity, and they are also exploiting and degrading nature. Global warming, the attenuation of the ozone shield, the menace of deforestation and desertification, the destruction of many species of flora and fauna, the extensive pollution of air, water and soil, and the poisoning of the food chain are threats that all people and societies have come to share in common.

There is no consensus as yet on how to tackle such mounting problems. The world around us is too new; we have not yet developed the personal and social cognitive maps to cope with it. The earlier maps are falling by the wayside at a vertiginous pace. We can no longer map our world as the struggle of capitalism and communism led by two superpowers; ours has become a more complex world, with more actors and different faces. The USSR has disappeared; the United States is preoccupied with economic problems at home. Japan's economic miracle is fading, and the "little dragons" of Asia are eager to take its place. Europe has become an economic but not political power, with its post-1992 single market and an East–West economic area of over 380 million people—and a Balkan rent by violence. Issues of environmental degradation are moving from marginal intellectual and youth groups to the center stage of international politics and global business. At the same time, many parts of the "Third World"—the 130-plus countries that count among themselves some three-quarters of the human population—sink further and further into poverty.

Adherence to the classical cognitive maps of the recent past is increasingly counterproductive—instead of the expected results, it produces surprises and shocks. This is true first of all in the area of the economy. The current variety of economic rationality legitimizes short-term policies that maximize competitiveness and profit and disregard the consequences of its actions in the medium and the long term. Some Third World governments are reluctant to pursue policies that reduce the ability of their national industries to compete and to produce—they would rather tolerate high levels of environmental degradation through chemical fertilizers, toxic-waste-dumping, and CFC-emission than put a brake on economic wealth-creation by ecological sanctions and regulations. Other governments perceive the need to bolster the global competitiveness of their economy by developing a dominant military presence in their region, legitimizing the acquisition of vast stockpiles of armaments by the search for economic security. Still other countries, with some industrial capacity but also considerable foreign debt, look to weapons-production as a means of coping with their trade deficits and increasing hard-currency exports. And still others export metals, minerals, timber, and other natural resources in response to pressures to obtain foreign currency, notwithstanding the fact that they are irreversibly depleting the wealth of their national patrimony.

GNP and other indicators of the economic wealth-creation process create an illusion that the natural resource-base of the economy is practically inexhaustible. In some cases, economic indicators suggest that wealth is actually increasing, even as natural resources are diminishing. If a government were to cut down all its forests and sell them as timber, its accounting books would report that its national wealth had increased; the same if it permitted pollution to become rampant and fought it by creating incentives for anti-pollution industries.

Because the long-term costs of such activities remain outside the accounting system as "externalities," factories can pollute rivers as if the waters that flowed past them entailed no costs; power stations can burn coal without calculating the cost of pumping carbon dioxide into the atmosphere; loggers can destroy wildlife and disrupt ecological cycles without factoring the costs into their balance sheets; and farmers can use chemical fertilizers, pesticides, and fuel-oil as though the self-regenerating capacity of the soil and the supply of fossil fuels were unlimited.

An obsolete cognitive map guides the operation of financial markets as well. There is, for example, the "Wall Street syndrome" of investing for short-term profit. Institutional investors, including managers of highly endowed mutual and pension funds, move around a great deal of capital in search of quick returns, deflecting funds from necessarily lower-yield socially and ecologically oriented projects.

There is yet another indication of the obsolescence of today's social cognitive maps, and that is the sectoral segmentation of the design and implementation of public policy. Governments act as if finance could be separated from trade, defense from development, and social justice from the degradation of the environment: they have departments or ministries attempting to cope with each such domain separately, often in direct competition with one another. Within the domain of the economy, they handle individual sectors as if finance dealt only with flows of money, trade only with flows of goods, and communication only with flows of messages. And they address environmental issues as if they were yet another specialty, assigning deforestation problems to forestry experts, soil-erosion issues to soil pathologists, atmospheric-pollution problems to chemists, and so on.

Dysfunctional social cognitive maps bias the actions of the international community as well. Financial flows are handled by the World Bank Group and the coordination apparatus established after World War II at Bretton Woods; security issues are assigned to the United Nations Security Council, and action in regard to the environment is entrusted to UNEP, the UN's environment program. Health issues have their own World Health Organization, and children their Unicef, just as weather has its World Meteorological Organization and the international mail system the International Postal Union. Even when an issue cuts across the fields of competence of several agencies—such as education, which, in addition to Unesco, is of concern to Unicef, UNDP, UNFPA, and half a dozen other UN bodies—the separation of mandates encourages bureaucratic narrow-mindedness and in-fighting, with the result that, instead of joining forces, territories are insistently claimed and jealously guarded, and the available funds are intensely fought for.

Despite labels such as "oneworld" and "spaceship Earth," an integrated and effective approach to the problems of our age still awaits realization. Governments, businesses, the same as private individuals, act as if the world was a jungle where the survival of one is the demise of another—but a large jungle, serving as an inexhaustible source of resources and an infinite sink of wastes. As a consequence, we find ourselves in a crisis in the Chinese sense of the term: in a condition replete with danger as well as with opportunity. If we are to avert the dangers and seize the opportunities, we need better to understand the real nature of this world; we need a more reality-matching cognitive map in societies, as well as in individuals.

Changes in Individual Cognitive Maps

As the first two chapters have shown, both individual and social cognitive maps have changed throughout history. Though the dominant maps are still in place, waves of change have started in recent years, moving strongly from the periphery toward the center. They wash over people and societies all over the world, in the rich as well as in the poor countries.

In the industrialized world, dominant values and beliefs have been shaped by the experience of the recent past, and as the realities of that world are changing, the concepts that mapped its contours are becoming increasingly obsolete. Serious changes started in the 1960s, at the periphery, with the Hippie, the New Age, and the early Green movements, and they kept moving toward center stage in the 1970s and 1980s with mounting concern over public health and safety, and worries over the negative effects of intensifying global economic competition. By the 1990s, the great majority of the industrialized societies had been caught up in what is sometimes referred to as a "paradigm shift." Since it is affecting the thinking and behavior of citizens as well as of consumers, governments as well as businesses are paying growing attention to it.

A profound change in the cognitive map of everyday people is now in the offing. Some old and cherished ideas are being rejected and replaced, and some basic relationships between humans and nature, as well as between humans and other humans, are being questioned. The changes are manifold; here is a brief but perhaps representative sample (Laszlo 1991).

• *The human–nature relationship.* The hitherto dominant cognitive map depicted human beings as mastering and controlling nature for their own ends. The emerging map calls attention to humanity as an organic part within the self-maintaining and self-evolving systems of nature in the planetary context of the biosphere.

- *The male–female relationship.* The mainstream map was male-dominated and hierarchical, conceiving of high concentrations of power and wealth as the best way to promote the interests and maintain the affluence of governments and enterprises. The emerging map places sharing and complementarity over top-down commands and blind obedience. It is orientated towards a male–female partnership, and is participatory rather than hierarchical.

- *Wholeness vs. fragmentation.* The cognitive map of the industrial age was atomistic and fragmented; it saw objects as separate from their environments, and people as separate from each other and replaceable in their surroundings. The emerging map perceives connections and communications between people, and between people and nature and emphasizes community and unity both in the natural and in the human world.

- *Competition vs. cooperation.* The cognitive map of classical industrial society looked at the economy as an arena for struggle and survival, and entrusted the coincidence of individual and public good to what Adam Smith called the "invisible hand." The alternative cognitive map emphasizes the value of cooperation over competition, and tempers the profit- and power-hunger of the modern work ethos with an appreciation of individuality and valuation of diversity.

- *Accumulating vs. sustaining.* In the map of the traditional industrial culture, the accumulation of material goods was considered the pinnacle of achievement and success; there was little concern with costs in terms of energies, raw materials, and related resources. The emerging map is becoming aware of the threats to the sustainability of the value-creating process, and is intent on flexibility and accommodation in the human–human as well as in the human–nature relationship.

These changes are part of a deeper shift in the worldview that underlies the cognitive map of contemporary people.

- The previous cognitive map of modern people was materialistic, seeing all things as distinct and measurable material entities. It conceptualized nature as a giant machine, composed of intricate but replaceable machine-like parts. The emerging cognitive map looks at nature as an organism endowed with irreplaceable elements and an innate but non-deterministic purpose, making for choice, for flow, and for spontaneity.

• In its application to society and the economy, the previous cognitive map highlighted the application of technology, the accumulation of material goods, and promoted a power-hungry, compete-to-win work ethos. The emerging cognitive map emphasizes the importance of information, and hence of education, communication and human services over and above technological fixes, the accumulation of material goods, and the control of people and nature.

• In the previous view, sickness was seen as the malfunction of a machine that could be best corrected by factual diagnosis and impersonal treatment; the ills of the mind were thought to be separable from those of the body, and were to be separately treated. In the alternative cognitive map, body and mind are not separable, and safeguarding the integrity and development of the whole organism requires empathy as well as expertise, and attention to psychological, social, and environmental factors in addition to physical and physiological conditions.

• In the spiritual domain, the previous concept envisaged the world as the work of a god who is outside, and indeed above and beyond his creation, with only humans privileged enough to be created in his image, to encounter his countenance, and to merit his love. The alternative cognitive map seeks the divine within all things natural, human, living, and even non-living, and refuses to draw categorical distinctions between the diverse spheres of reality.

• The previous view was globalizing and hierarchical, conceiving of high concentrations of power and wealth as the best way to maintain and promote the interests and affluence of states and corporations. The emerging cognitive map is likewise globally oriented, but in a participatory rather than in a hierarchical vein. It places cooperation born of understanding over top-down commands and blind obedience.

• Last but not least, the previous cognitive map of people was Eurocentric, looking at Western industrialized societies as the paradigms of progress; the cognitive map that is now dawning is centered on humanity.

A number of traditional conceptions and preconceptions are not only questioned, but are actually replaced by new insights. It is widely admitted, for example,

- that in this world those who survive are not necessarily those who are the strongest, but those who are the most symbiotic with their fellow humans and the systems of nature;

- that the trickle-down theory is a myth, and the only way to help the poor and the underprivileged is to create better conditions for their life and better opportunities for their advancement through higher levels of participation in economic, social and political processes;

- that specialists who know more and more about less and less need to be balanced by generalists who have sufficient overview to see the forest and not only a multiplicity of trees, and therefore make better guides in today's complex and interdependent world;

- that true efficiency is not simply maximum productivity but the creation of socially useful and necessary goods and services;

- and that ideas, values, and beliefs are not idle playthings but have a vital catalytic role in the world, not only in producing technological innovations but, even more importantly, by paving the way for the social and cultural advances that are the basic precondition of progress in the current transition toward a new world in the twenty-first century.

Changes in Social Cognitive Maps

In the political sphere, the mutation of the dominant cognitive map came late, but then it came forcefully. Until about 1988, ecopolitics was not popular in government circles. The governments of the industrialized countries underplayed environmental issues, fearing negative impacts on economic growth and global competitiveness. The former Marxist regimes of Eastern Europe had rejected ecological measures outright: there could be no environmental degradation under socialism. In turn, the governments of the developing countries claimed that environmental problems are due to pollution produced by the industrialized nations, and those nations should shoulder the responsibility for overcoming them.

Then, in 1988, the public media in the industrialized world seized on the environment as a topic of major public interest. Within a single year, the National Geographic Society published *Earth '88, Time* magazine devoted its 1989 New Year's edition to "Earth, Planet of the Year," *The Economist* published a special survey on "Costing the Earth," *Scientific American* dedicated an issue to "Managing Planet Earth," and *The New Yorker* published a 35-page article on "The End of Nature."

Public opinion began to come around, and politicians were quick to note the changed mood of their electorate. Almost half of Margaret Thatcher's September 1988 speech to the Royal Society was devoted to the issue of environmental imbalances and the need to accept the concept of sustainable economic development. In his December 1988 speech to the UN, Mikhail Gorbachev spoke of the ecological catastrophe that would follow on traditional types of industrialization. Queen Beatrix of the Netherlands dedicated her entire Christmas speech to the nation to environmental threats confronting life on earth. And George Bush appointed professional environmentalist and former president of the World Wildlife Fund William Reilly to his cabinet, as Administrator of the Environmental Protection Agency (EPA).

Related changes have been occurring in the cognitive map of business, surfacing as the "new corporate culture." They concern issues such as:

- *Hierarchical vs. distributed decision-making.* The philosophy of the classical corporation was to create a disciplined hierarchy in which top managers decided all the essential parameters of the organization's activity. The new corporate culture moves toward decentralizing decision-making through network-like structures in which people closest to a given problem have the task and the responsibility of making the day-to-day decisions.

- *Control vs. self-regulation.* Old-style management applied rigorous external controls in all phases of work, making use of supervisors, specialists, and automated control procedures. The new style relies on self-regulation by semi-autonomous task-groups and broadly networked subdivisions.

- *Human vs. machine.* Classical management viewed the human being as an extension of the machine, and whenever possible substituted "reliable" machines for "unreliable" people. The emerging corporate culture views the human being as an uneliminable and vital complement to machines, and as irreplaceable by automation in all phases of business activity.

- *Routine tasks vs. responsible jobs.* The old-style corporation broke down tasks into simple and narrow-range skills, mechanizing the work process in the way Charlie Chaplin caricatured in *Modern Times.* The new corporation makes use of semi-autonomous task-groups and optimizes their contribution by assigning broad responsibilities to them, corresponding to their multiple skills and many-sided performance.

- *Complementary sex roles.* Mainstream corporate culture typically viewed women as unskilled or semi-skilled labor, and assigned simple or routine tasks to them—on the assembly-line, in cleaning up, and in routine secretarial jobs. The new corporate culture brings women into all levels of decision-making; it recognizes the complementarity of male and female personalities, skills, and concerns.

The fact is that, in the last few years, an entire new industry has been arising. It deals with biodegradable and organic products, environmentally harmless substances, the recycling of reusable materials, and the clean-up of existing pollution. By 1991, the US "Earth Age Industry" generated over US$100 billion in turnover and employed some 200,000 people.

Not surprisingly, the top management of globally operating transnational corporations now includes directors for environmental affairs. By 1990, one hundred percent of Dutch international companies, and the majority of German and Japanese companies, had a board member entrusted with environmental responsibilities. In some industry sectors, chief executives now devote as much as a third of their time to ecological issues, and many companies undertake costly alterations in product-design and manufacturing to meet self-imposed ecological standards.

The Evolutionary Map of the Sciences

In our science-infused and technology-dominated world, the contribution of science to the creation of a new and more adequate cognitive map remains essential. Science is a major—perhaps *the* major—force shaping contemporary industrial civilization. The revolutions of our time are driven by the social and technological implications of scientific breakthroughs rather than by the will of politicians or dictators. Scientific discoveries are extending the human life span, making it possible to reduce working hours and increase leisure-time, and to travel anywhere on the six continents in a matter of hours in considerable comfort and safety. Scientific discoveries are also bringing to our fingertips ideas, images, and information on practically everything, from local events to global problems, in every conceivable field of public and personal interest.

At the same time, the products of industrial technologies are altering vital balances in the biosphere, changing the chemical composition of soil, water, and air, and wreaking havoc with the global climate; and the elemental power liberated by nuclear science, stockpiled in national arsenals, is endangering all life on the surface of this planet. Breakthroughs in microelectronics make for the quasi-instantaneous processing of a staggering amount of information, and the distribution of the information quasi-instantaneously to almost anyone, anywhere on the globe, while breakthroughs in biotechnologies make possible the manipulation of the genetic heritage of our species, with untold consequences for good as well as for bad.

Despite the shifts in values and worldviews already noted, the view of the world conveyed by scientific discoveries remains unclear to most people. Misconceptions about the nature of the cognitive map elaborated by science lead to mistaken applications and misguided practices. To this day, the absolutist and mechanistic worldview of Newtonian physics dominates interventions in society and in nature; most leaders believe that the world can be engineered to suit human wishes, much like the structure of a building or a bridge. The concepts of classical Darwinism inspired Hitler's social Darwinism and still underlie attempts to govern according to the principle that only might is right. Power and wealth can still be looked upon as signs of fitness; poverty and marginalization as signs of being a misfit. Even Einstein's theories have been misinterpreted to mean that everything is relative, including freedom, health, justice, and morality.

It is noteworthy, then, that for the past decade or so, an increasing number of scientists have been at pains to clarify a very different and in some respects diametrically opposite cognitive map suggested by the latest discoveries in the sciences. The new physics and the new cosmology, and the new sciences of nature and complexity, elaborate and specify the vision of a self-evolving, dynamic, and essentially unified reality in which life and mind, and human beings and human societies, are not strangers or accidents but integral co-evolving elements.

Today mathematical physicists, and not only poets and philosophers, are attempting to produce an integrated evolutionary map of the world. Many scientists have been fascinated by the notion that there is a vantage point from which the 200-odd elementary particles and the four universal forces of nature can be seen as evolving from a single "supergrand unified" force—the force that is the origin of all that is. Ten or twenty three-dimensional universes, Big Bangs, black holes, supersymmetries, and superstrings are strange notions that scientists do not hesitate to espouse to prove the unity of the universe in theories that have come to be popularly known as TOEs—"theories of everything."

As physicists have been turning their eyes to the cosmos, the public has been turning its eyes to the new physics. Stephen Hawking's *Brief History of Time* sold over a million copies; James Gleick's *Chaos: Making of a New Science* made the bestseller lists. One large Manhattan bookstore devoted an entire window to new books on physics and cosmology; another displayed Paul Davies' *The Cosmic Blueprint* next to the latest collection of "Garfield" cartoons; and Bantam science editor Leslie Meredith declared that we are entering science's golden age.

In the new sciences, a new and different picture of the world has indeed been emerging: a highly unified picture. In this picture, the particles and forces of the physical universe originate from a single "supergrand unified force" and, although separating into distinct dynamic events, they continue to interact. Space–time is a dynamic continuum in which all particles and forces are integral elements. Every particle, every element affects every other. There are no external forces or separate things, only sets of interacting actualities with differentiated characteristics.

The new physicists have given up trying to explain the world in terms of laws of motion governing the behavior of individual particles. A coherent and consistent set of abstract and unvisualizable entities has replaced the classical notion of passive material atoms moving under the influence of external forces. This is important, because it is unlikely that phenomena of the level of complexity typical of life could be described by equations that center uniquely on the motion of the universe's smallest building blocks, no matter how thoroughly these entities and their laws are unified. A focus on a basic level of reality is unnecessary baggage left over from a classical theory that attempted to explain all things in reference to a combination of the properties of ultimate entities—entities that it has long believed to be atoms. The new scientists no longer maintain that nature can be explained in terms of groups of fundamental entities, even if the entities are not atoms but quarks, exchange particles, or strings.

The cognitive map emerging in the new physics is that of a universe that is whole and self-organizing. This map is likely to remain valid, notwithstanding the high attrition rate of the hypotheses that expound it. It is difficult to see how science would ever regress to a universe of separate material things and dynamic forces, to a mosaic of unrelated events in mechanical equilibrium.

To have a good map of the world does not require having a map of *every thing* in the world; it only calls for having a sound grasp of the fundamental nature of the *processes* by which every thing that is in the world *came to be*. This is the essence of the emerging evolutionary map.

Let us retrace our steps, now, to the beginnings of the cosmic process some fifteen billion years ago. That was the epoch of universe creation by the primal explosion that became popularly known as the *Big Bang*. Although cosmologists disagree on the details of the process, it is clear that the universe we now observe had a beginning in time, and that since that beginning it has continued to evolve toward the order and complexity that now meets our eye.

Imagine, if you will, a cosmos of pure structure without things and movement. It is a "hypervacuum" made up of pure, potential energy. Except for tiny fluctuations, it is quiescent and unimaginably concentrated. Then one of the fluctuations suddenly nucleates and the pinpoint universe explodes. Within the smallest fraction of a second, the structure becomes fiery, and inflates to billions of times its former size. It begins to fly apart, and as it expands it cools. The continuous field of potential energy breaks up at myriad critical points, and nodules of real, actualized energy spring forth. The nodules have opposite charges, and as they meet they annihilate each other. Some survive, and establish themselves in space and time. Now there is something there: the material universe has been born. The nodules of persistent actualized energies bind together and form larger patterns that endure in time and repeat in space. "Things" emerge from the background of potential energies like knots on a fishing net, and they interact across the expanding substructure, contorting it by their presence. They are, in Einstein's theory, "electromagnetic disturbances" in the matrix of four-dimensional space–time.

Let us suppose that there are a vast number of such knots tied across the reaches of space–time, and that these knots are at uneven distances from one another. They do not form isolated units but parts of a continuum, and they communicate with one another through the continuum. Their primary mode of communication is attraction and repulsion, depending on the distance that separates them from one another. Attraction is the dominant mode of communication at all but extremely close intervals, and thus the knots in relative proximity move closer together. Many of them come to be concentrated in such close quarters that ordinary attraction breaks down and more complex strains and stresses are created between them. Some of the elementary units achieve cohesion in balancing the energy flows that constitute them in a joint pattern. They constitute "superknots" of a much more complex kind.

A population of such complex entities transforms the character of space–time in the region of their concentration. There arises a material object—a star. These macro-objects continue to be connected through the continuum on which they are superimposed, but now they act as integrated masses: they form complexes constituted by the balance of their joint attractions and repulsions. The relatively stable superunits thus emerging further associate among themselves. Eventually, the entire universe is dotted with balanced knots-within-knots in space–time, affecting each other and reaching further orders of delicate balance. The universe itself takes on the character of a vast system of balanced energies, acting in some discernible form of cohesion. Thus the whole universe expands, or expands and then re-contracts, or maintains itself in a dynamic steady-state—we are not sure which, at this stage of theoretical cosmology.

In some cosmic regions—such as on planetary surfaces—further processes of structuration occur. Neighboring nodules interact and accommodate one another's internal flow-patterns. The new integration of already-integrated energies results in more complex flows along relatively stable pathways. The pathways themselves are the result of previous integrations; they themselves consist of energy-flows of established pattern. But now they serve to channel fresh flows of energy, and act as "structure" in relation to "function." Hence, new waves of formative energy course over stabilized structures, produced by foregoing waves. And the process continues; the beat goes on. Established structures jointly constitute new pathways and these, as they become established as structures in time, serve as templates for the production of new systems of flows. The patterns become complex; the cosmic cathedral of systems grows.

The known entities of science are interfaces located on various levels of the rising cathedral.

Electrons and nucleons are condensations of energies in the space–time field, based on the integration of quarks. They in turn are capable of integration into balanced structures: stable atoms. Here, the integration of diverse forces within the nucleus produces a positive energy, which is matched by the summed negative energy of the electrons in the surrounding shells. Uncompleted shells make the atom chemically active; that is, capable of forming bonds with neighboring atoms. We thus get systems produced by the integration of the energies of several atoms: chemical molecules. The tremendous potentials of electronic bonding, as well as of weaker forces of association, permit the formation of complex polymer molecules and of crystals, under energetically favorable conditions. In some regions, under especially favorable conditions, the level of organization reaches that of enormously heavy organic substances, such as protein molecules and nucleic acids. Now the basic building blocks are given for the constitution of self-replicating units of still higher organizational level: cells. These systems maintain a constant flow of substances through their structures, imposing on it a steady-state with specific parameters. The inputs and outputs may achieve coordination with analogous units in the surrounding medium, and we are on our way toward multicellular phenomena.

The resulting structures (organisms) are likewise steady-state patterns imposed on a continuous flow, this time of free energies, substances (rigidly integrated energies), and information (coded patterns of energies). The input–output channels of organisms can further solidify into pathways of definite structure, and the nature of these pathways, plus the variety of locally interacting organic systems, defines the ecological system. In some instances, where highly interacting organisms congregate, the pathways cohere into a system made up of but one variety of organism: this is a social system. And where the interacting organisms are conscious, symbol-using creatures, the system that emerges in the wake of their intercourse is sociocultural. Ultimately the strands of communication and interaction straddle the space–time region in which they occur and form a system of their own. This is Gaia, the system of the global bio- and sociosphere.

Here, then, is an evolutionary vision of the largest "forest" of all, the cosmos in its totality. Visions of this scope were once the province of poets and mystics, and perhaps of theologians and metaphysicians, but certainly not of scientists. Not so today. As we have just seen, a basically unified cognitive map is emerging today in the laboratories and workshops of the new physics, the new biology, the new ecology, and the avant-garde branches of the social and historical sciences. The new evolutionary map is practical and applicable: focusing on the forest does not prevent anyone from seeing the trees.

Practical Utility of the Emerging Evolutionary Map

The new cognitive map of the sciences offers a powerful way to look at the world; a way that can promote effective and responsible behavior.

As early as 1975, Erich Jantsch noted that the reward for the elaboration of an evolutionary vision will be not only an improved academic understanding of how we are interconnected with evolutionary dynamics at all levels of reality, but also an immensely practical philosophy to guide us in a time of creative instability and major restructuration of the human world. Jonas Salk (1972) affirmed in turn that having become conscious of evolution, we must now make evolution itself conscious. And in *The New Evolutionary Paradigm*, David Loye outlined the foreseeable basic benefits of the development of a natural-science-based evolutionary cognitive map in regard to society.

1. *The benefits of improved forecasting.* While the study of evolution through chaos in the natural sciences has uncovered specific limits for predictability during transitional states, it is now also discovering new possibilities for improving forecasting within these limits by identifying patterns that foreshadow either impending chaos or potential order out of chaos. The new advances suggest how more effective early-warning systems may be developed for identifying impending food, financial, political, and environmental crises. The need for such systems became crystal clear when, basically unprepared, the leaders of the international community faced the great waves of system transformation that began mid-century with decolonization in the Third World, continued in the 1990s with the dissolution of the Second, and led to the series of crises in the 1990s, including the wars in the Persian Gulf, in Somalia, and in Bosnia.

2. *The benefits of improved interventional guides.* As important for effective and responsible behavior as the forecasting of impending crises and transformations is the identification of fruitful routes that could lead out of the crises. Indeed, one of the greatest problems faced by people in decision-making positions today is knowing where, when, and how to intervene to prevent social, economic, political, or ecological crises— or, if prevention is no longer possible, how to alleviate and ultimately overcome the crises. The new cognitive map holds out an important promise in this regard: mathematically formulated dynamic systems theories enable the creation of computer graphics that allow scientists to reduce vast quantities of otherwise confusing data into a comprehensible form. This can simplify the understanding and communication of problems and the visualization of swift and effective intervention

strategies to overcome them. According to Ralph Abraham (1992), evolutionary modeling—especially in the form known as *modular dynamics*—can provide contemporary civilization with the means to transcend coming crises.

3. *The benefits of participatory rather than authoritarian problem-solutions.* The traditional recipe during times of trouble has been to turn to specialized experts for advice and to implement the advice through top-down authoritarian strategies. As the failed Soviet coup of August 1991 has shown, attempted solutions that disregard the participation and motivation of the wider masses whose life and well-being are affected exacerbate the problems they were meant to solve and create a new range of difficulties. The promise of the new cognitive map in this regard is that it permits broad segments of the population to share the concept underlying the proposed solutions. Hence, the new map could bring about a wide level of public comprehension of both problems and proposed solutions.

4. *The benefits of providing clearer long-term goals and humanistic images.* Futurists and social scientists have remarked that, in contrast to the fervent visions of a better future that animated the revolutions and re-forms of the eighteenth and nineteenth centuries, in the present century a confused and fearful humanity seems to be running out of positive vision. Romantic utopias have been dismissed as unscientific, the Marxist vision has failed, and visions inspired by religious tenets seem too otherworldly to motivate practical strategies. The utility of the emerging evolutionary cognitive map includes the promise of rectifying this situation. When adequately articulated and widely understood, it could revitalize currently atrophying images of the future and recharge public motivation in reaching for long-term objectives that are humanistic in intent and realistic in attainment.

Bibliography

Abraham, R. (1989). Social synergy and international synergy: A mathematical model. *IS Journal, 17*, 27–31.

——(1992). Mathematical cooperation. In A. L. Combs (Ed.), *Cooperation: Reaching for a new order* (pp. 68–75). New York: Gordon & Breach.

Anderson, T. W. (1990). *Reality isn't what it used to be.* San Francisco, CA: Harper & Row.

Artigiani, R. (1988). Scientific revolution and the evolution of consciousness. *World Futures: The Journal of General Evolution, 25*(3–4), 237–281.

——(1990). Post-modernism and social evolution: An enquiry. *World Futures: The Journal of General Evolution, 30*(3), 149–163.

Augros, R., & Stanciu, G. (1987). *The new biology: Discovering the wisdom in nature.* Boston: Shambhala.

—— ——(1992). Competition and enculturation in science. In A. L. Combs (Ed.), *Cooperation: Reaching for a new order.* New York: Gordon & Breach.

Bandura, A. (1989). Social cognitive theory. In R. Vasta (Ed.), *Annals of child development: Vol. 6. Six theories of child development: Revised formulations and current issues.* Greenwich, CT: JAI Press.

Barnett, S. A., & Cowan, P. E. (1976). Activity, exploration, curiosity and fear. *Interdisciplinary Scientific Review, 1*, 43–62.

Bateson, B. (1972). *Steps to an ecology of mind.* New York: Ballantine.

Beritashvili, I. S. (1971). *Vertebrate memory, characteristics and origin.* New York: Plenum Press.

Berthoff, R., & Murrin, J. M. (1973). Feudalism, communalism and the yeoman freeholder. In S. G. Kurtz & J. H. Hutson (Eds.), *Essays on the American Revolution.* Chapel Hill, NC: University of North Carolina Press.

Beusekom, G. van. (1946). *Over de Orientate van de Bijenwolf (Philanthus triangulatum Fabre).* Leiden.

Boulding, K. (1956). *The image.* Ann Arbor, MI: University of Michigan Press.

Bruner, J. S., Olver, R. O., & Greenfield, P. M. (1966). *Studies in cognitive growth.* New York: Wiley.

Campbell, J. (1988). *Historical atlas of world mythology: Vol. 1. The way of the animal powers: Part 1. Mythologies of the primitive hunters and gathers.* New York: Harper & Row.

Camus, A. (1956). *The rebel: An essay on man in revolt* (A. Bower, Trans.). New York: A. A. Knopf.

Chance, M. R. A. (Ed.). (1988). *Social fabrics of the mind.* Hillsdale, NJ: Lawrence Erlbaum.

Chatwin, B. (1988). *The songlines.* New York: Viking Penguin.

Childe, V. G. (1951). *Man makes himself.* New York: Mentor.

Cole, S., Hainsworth, R., Kamil, A. C., Mercier, T., & Wolf, L. L. (1982). Spatial learning as an adaptation in hummingbirds. *Science, 217,* 655–657.

Combs, A. C., & Holland, M. (1990). *Synchronicity: Science, myth and the trickster.* New York: Paragon House.

Connerton, P. (1989). *How societies remember.* Cambridge: Cambridge University Press.

Cowie, R. J., Krebs, J. R., & Sherry, D. (1981). Food storing by marsh tits. *Animal Behavior, 29,* 1252–1255.

Craik, K. (1943). *The nature of explanation.* Cambridge: Cambridge University Press.

Croze, H. (1970). Searching image in carrion crows. *Zeitsrift for Tierpsychology, 5,* 1–86.

Csányi, V. (1986). How is the brain modelling the environment? A case study by the paradise fish. In G. Montalenti and G. Tecce (Eds.), *Variability and behavioral evolution: Proceedings, Accademia Nazionale dei Lincei, 259,* 142–157.

——(1987). The replicative evolutionary model of animal and human minds. *World Futures: The Journal of General Evolution, 24*(3), 174–214.

——(1988a). *Evolutionary systems and society: A general theory of life, mind, and culture.* Durham, NC: Duke University Press.

——(1988b). Contribution of the genetical and neural memory to animal intelligence. In H. Jerison and I. Jerison (Eds.), *Intelligence and Evolutionary Biology* (pp. 299–318). Berlin: Springer-Verlag.

——(1989). Origin of complexity and organizational levels during evolution. In D. B. Wake & G. Roth (Eds.), *Complex organizational functions* (pp. 349–360). London: John Wiley & Sons.

——(1990). The shift from group cohesion to idea cohesion is a major step in cultural evolution. *World Futures: The Journal of General Evolution, 29,* 1–8.

——(1992). The brain's models and communication. In T. A. Sebeok & J. Umiker-Sebeok (Eds.), *The Semiotic Web.* Berlin: Moyton de Gruyter.

Curio, E., Ernst, U., & Vieth, W. (1978). Cultural transmission of enemy recognition. *Science, 202,* 899–901.

Davies, P. C. W. (1988). *The cosmic blueprint: New discoveries in nature's creative ability to order the universe.* New York: Simon and Schuster.

Dawkins, M. (1971). Perceptual changes in chicks: Another look at the search image concept. *Animal Behavior, 19,* 566–574.

Douglas, M. (1986). *How institutions think.* Cambridge: Cambridge University Press.

Douglas-Hamilton, I. O. (1976). *Among the elephants.* New York: Viking Press.

Downs, R. W., & Stea, D. (Eds.). (1973). *Image and environment.* London: Edward Arnold.

Drager, U. C., & Hubel, D. H. (1975). Responses to visual stimulation and relationship between visual, auditory and somatosensory inputs in mouse superior colliculus. *Journal of Neurophysiology, 38,* 690–713.

Eccles, J. C. (1989). *Evolution of the brain: Creation of the mind.* New York: Routledge.

Eibl-Eibesfeldt, I. (1970). *Ethology: The biology of behavior.* New York: Holt, Rinehart and Winston.

——(1989). *Human ethology.* New York: Aldine de Gruyter.

Eisler, R. (1987). *The chalice and the blade: Our history, our future.* San Francisco, CA: Harper & Row.

——(1995). *Sacred pleasures: Sex, myth, and the politics of the body.* San Francisco, CA: HarperSanFrancisco.

——& Loye, D. (1990). *The partnership way: New tools for living and learning, healing our families, our communities, and our world.* San Francisco, CA: Harper Collins.

Engels, F. (1972). *The origin of the family, private property and the state* (Ed. E. Leacock). London: Lawrence & Wishart. (Original work published 1884)

Ewert, J. P. (1980). *Neuroethology.* Berlin: Springer-Verlag.

Fentress, J., & Wickham, C. (1992). *Social memory.* Cambridge, MA: Blackwell.

Fox, R. L. (1992). *The unauthorized version.* New York: Knopf.

Frankfort, H. (1973). *Before philosophy.* Baltimore, MD: Penguin.

Fromm, E. (1947). *Man for himself: An inquiry into the psychology of ethics.* New York: Holt, Rinehart and Winston.

Galef, B. G., Jr. (1976). The social transmission of acquired behavior: A discussion of tradition and social learning in vertebrates. *Advances in the Study of Behavior, 6,* 77–100.

Gazzaniga, M. S. (1985). *The social brain: Discovering the networks of the mind.* New York: Basic Books.

Gibson, J. J. (1966). *The senses considered as a perceptual system.* Boston, MA: Houghton-Mifflin.

Gilligan, C. (1982). *In a different voice: Psychological theory and women's development.* Cambridge, MA: Harvard University Press.

Gimbutas, M. (1982). *The goddesses and gods of old Europe.* Los Angeles, CA: University of California Press.

Gladwin, T. (1970). *East is a big bird.* Cambridge, MA: Harvard University Press.

Gleick, J. (1987). *Chaos: Making a new science.* New York: Viking.

Globus, G. (1987a). Three holonomic approaches to the brain. In B. Hiley & D. Peat (Eds.), *Quantum implications.* London: Routledge & Kegan Paul.

——(1987b). *Dream life, wake life: The human condition through dreams.* Albany, NY: State University of New York Press.

Goffman, I. (1973). *The presentation of self in everyday life.* Woodstock: Overlook Press.

Goody, J. (1977). *The domestication of the savage mind.* Cambridge: Cambridge University Press.

Hacking, I. (1985). *Restructuring individualism.* Stanford, CA: Stanford University Press.

Hawking, S. W. (1988). *A brief history of time.* New York: Bantam.

Hediger, H. (1976). Proper names in the animal kingdom. *Experientia, 32,* 1357–1488.

Hinde, R. A. and Fischer, J. (1952). Further observations on the opening of milk bottles by birds. *British Birds, 44,* 306–311.

Hofstadter, D. R. (1979). *Gödel, Esher, Bach: An eternal golden braid.* New York: Basic Books.

Jacob, F. (1982). *The possible and the actual.* New York: Pantheon.

James, W. (1983). *The principles of psychology.* Cambridge, MA: Harvard University Press. (Original work published 1890)

Jantsch, E. (1975). *Design for evolution: Self-organization and planning in the life of human systems.* New York: George Braziller.

Jay, M. (1973). *The dialectical imagination.* Boston: Little-Brown.

Jaynes, J. (1976). *The origin of consciousness in the breakdown of the bicameral mind.* Boston, MA: Houghton Mifflin.

Jerison, H. J. (1973). *The evolution of the brain and intelligence.* New York: Academic Press.

Jouventin, P. (1982). *Visual and vocal signals in penguins, their evolution and adaptive characters.* Berlin: Verlag P. Parley.

Jung, C. G. (1959). *Flying saucers: A modern myth of things seen in the skies.* New York.

——(1961). *Dreams, memories, reflections.* New York: Random House.

Kahler, E. (1956). *Man the measure: A new approach to history.* New York: George Braziller.

Kamil, A. C. and Balda, R. P. (1985). Cache recovery and spatial memory in Clark's Nutcrackers (*Nucifraga columbiana*). *Journal of Experimental Psychology and Animal Behavior, Proceedings, 11,* 95–111.

Kauffman, S. A. (1993). *The origins of order: Self-organization and selection in evolution.* New York & Oxford: Oxford University Press.

Kawai, M. (1965). Newly acquired precultural behavior of the natural troops of Japanese monkeys on Koshima Island. *Primates, 6,* 1–30.

Kendrick, K. M. and Baldwin, B. A. (1987). Cells in temporal cortex of conscious sheep can respond preferentially to the sight of faces. *Science, 2436,* 448–450.

Kierkegaard, S. (1954). *Fear and trembling, and The sickness unto death.* (Walter Lowrie, Trans.). Garden City, NY: Doubleday Anchor. (Original work published 1849)

Knudsen, E. I. (1981). The hearing of the barn owl. *Scientific American, 245*(6), 82–91.

Kohlberg, L. (1984). *The psychology of moral development.* New York: Harper & Row.

Korzybski, A. (1958). *Science and sanity: An introduction to non-Aristotelian systems and general semantics.* 4th edn. Shore, CT: Institute of General Semantics.

Kosslyn, S. M. (1980). *Image and mind.* Cambridge, MA: Harvard University Press.

Lack, D. 1939. The display of the blackcock. *British Birds, 32,* 290–303.

Laszlo, E. (1987a). *Evolution: The grand synthesis.* Boston: Shambhala.

——(1987b). The psi-field hypothesis. *IS Journal, 4,* 13–28.

——(1991). *The age of bifurcation: Understanding the changing world.* New York: Gordon & Breach.

——(1993). *The creative universe: Toward a unified science of matter, life and mind.* Edinburgh: Floris.

——(1994). *The choice: Evolution or extinction.* Los Angeles, CA: Tarcher/ Putnam.

——(1995). *The connected universe.* London: World Scientific.

Leider, D. (1990). *The absent body.* Chicago, IL: University of Chicago Press.

Lickona, T. (1983). *Raising good children.* New York: Bantam.

Lovelock, J. E. (1979). *Gaia: A new look at life on Earth.* Oxford: Oxford University Press.

Loye, D. (1983). *The sphinx and the rainbow.* Boulder, CO: Shambhala.

——(1990). Moral sensitivity and the evolution of higher mind. *World Futures: The Journal of General Evolution, 30,* 41–52.

——(forthcoming). *The glacier and the flame: Of science and moral sensitivity.*

Lumann, N. (1986). *Love as passion.* Cambridge, MA: Harvard University Press.

Luria, A. (1966). *The human brain and psychological processes.* New York: Harper & Row.

Lynch, K. (1960). *The image of the city.* Cambridge, MA: Harvard University Press.

McFarland, D. J. (1985). *Animal behaviour.* London: Pitman.

MacKay, D. M. (1951). Mindlike behavior of artifacts. *British Journal of Philosophy of Science, 2,* 105–121.

Mandler, J. M. (1988). How to build a baby: On the development of an accessible representation system. *Cognitive development, 3,* 113–136.

Mann, M. (1986). *The sources of social power.* Cambridge: Cambridge University Press.

Maslow, A. H. (1965). *Eupsychian management.* Homewood, IL: Irwin.

——& Honigmann, J. J. (1970). Synergy: Some notes of Ruth Benedict. *American Anthropologist, 72,* 320–333.

Maturana, H. R., Lettvin, J. Y., McCulloch, W. S., & Pitts, W. H. (1960). Anatomy and physiology of vision in the frog (*Rana pipiens*). *J. Gen. Physiol., 43* (Suppl. 6), 129–175.

——& Varela, F. J. (1987). *The tree of knowledge: The biological roots of human understanding.* Boston, MA: Shambhala.

————& Uribe, R. (1974). Autopoiesis: The organization of living systems, its characterization and model. *Biosystems, 5,* 187–196.

Menzel, E. W. (1978). Cognitive mapping in chimpanzee. In S. H. Hulse, H.

Fower, & W. K. Honig (Eds.), *Cognitive Processes in Animal Behavior* (pp. 375–422). Hillsdale, NJ: Lawrence Erlbaum.

Mundinger, P. C. (1980). Animal cultures and a general theory of cultural evolution. *Ethology and Sociobiology, 1*, 183–223.

Murray, G. (1951). *The five stages of Greek religion.* Garden City, NY: Doubleday Anchor.

Neisser, U. (1976). *Cognition and reality.* San Francisco, CA: W. H. Freeman.

——(Ed). (1982). *Memory observed: Remembering in natural contexts.* San Francisco, CA: W. H. Freeman.

Nicolis, J. N. (1986). *The dynamics of hierarchical systems.* New York: Springer-Verlag.

Norton-Griffiths, M. (1969). The organization, control and development of parental feeding in the oystercatcher (*Haematopus ostralegus*). *Behaviour, 24,* 55–114.

Olton, D. S., and Samuelson, R. J. (1976). Remembrance of places past: Spatial memory in rats. *Journal of Experimental Psychology and Animal Behavior, Proceedings, 2,* 97–116.

Payne, T. L. 1974. Pheromone perception. In M. C. Birch (Ed.), *Pheromones.* Amsterdam: North Holland.

Perret, D. I., Smith, P. A. J., Potter, D. D., Mistlin, A. J., Head, A. S., Milner, A. D., & Jeeves, M. (1985). Visual cells in the temporal cortex sensitive to face view and gaze direction. *Proceedings of the Royal Society of London, B223,* 293–317.

Piaget, J. (1965). *The moral judgment of the child.* New York: Free Press.

——& Inhelder, B. (1971). *Mental imagery in the child.* New York: Basic Books.

Popper, K. R. (1962). *The open society and its enemies.* New York: Harper Torchbooks.

Pribram, K. H. (1991). *Brain and perception: Holonomy and structure in figural processing.* Hillsdale, NJ: Lawrence Erlbaum.

Reich, W. (1972). *Sex-pol: Essays, 1929–1934.* New York: Vintage.

Reilly, K. (1980). *The West and the world.* New York: Harper & Row.

Roeder, K. D., & Treat, A. E. (1961). The detection and evasion of bats by moths. *American Scientist, 49,* 135–148.

Rogers, C. R. (1961). *On becoming a person.* Boston, MA: Houghton-Mifflin.

Roitblat, H. L., Tham, W., & Golub, L. (1982). Performance of *Betta splendens* in a radial arm maze. *Animal Learning and Behavior, 10,* 108–114.

Sackett, G. P. (1966). Monkeys reared in isolation with pictures as visual input: Evidence for an innate releasing mechanism. *Science, 1954,* 1468–1473.

Sasvári, L. 1979. Observational learning in great marsh and blue tits. *Animal Behavior, 27,* 767–771.

Schleidt, W. M., Schleidt, M., & Magg, M. (1960). Störungen der Mutter-Kind-Beziehung bei Truthünern durch Gehörverlust. *Behaviour, 16,* 254–260.

Schmandt-Besserat, D. (1986). The origins of writing. *Written Communication, 3*(1), 31–45.

Schmookler, A. B. (1984). *The parable of the tribes: The problem of power in social evolution.* Berkeley, CA: University of California Press.

Schneirla, T. C. (1953). Modifiability in insect behavior. In K. D. Roeder (Ed.), *Insect Physiology* (pp. 723–747). New York: John Wiley & Sons.

Schwartz, G. (1984). *Psychology of learning and memory.* London: W. W. Norton.

Seitz, A. (1940). Paarbildung bei einigen Cichliden I. *Zeitsrift for Tierpsychology,* 4, 40–84.

Sheldrake, R. (1987). Part I: Mind, memory and archetypes: Morphic resonance and the collective unconscious. *Psychological Perspectives, 18*(1), 9–25.

Suga, N., Kuzirai, K., & O'Neill, W. E. (1981). How biosonar information is represented in the bat cerebral cortex. In J. Syka and L. Aitkin (Eds.), *Neuronal mechanisms of hearing* (pp. 197–219). New York: Plenum Press.

Taylor, C. (1989). *Sources of the self.* Cambridge, MA: Harvard University Press.

Thoma, S. J. (1986). Estimating gender differences in the comprehension and preference of moral issues. *Developmental Review, 6,* 165–180.

Tinbergen, N. (1932). Über die Orientiering des Bienenwolfes (*Philanthus triangulum*). *Zs. vergl. Physiol., 21,* 699–716.

——(1951). *The study of instinct.* London: Oxford University Press.

——(1960). *The herring gull's world.* New York: Harper & Row.

——& Kruyt, W. (1938). Über die Orientierung des Bienenwolfes (*Philantus triangulum Fabr.*) III: Die Bevorzugung bestimmter Wegmarken. *Zs. vergl. Physiol., 25,* 292–334.

Tolman, E. C. (1932). *The purposive behaviour in animals and men.* New York: Appleton.

——(1948). Cognitive maps in rats and men. *Psychological Review, 55,* 189–209.

Toulmin, S. (1990). *Cosmopolis: The hidden agenda of modernity.* New York: Free Press.

Turner, V. (1986). *The anthropology of performance.* New York: PAJ.

Uexkuell, J. von 1934. *Streifzüge durch die Umwelten von Tieren und Menschen.* Berlin: Springer-Verlag.

Uttal, W. R. (1972). *The psychobiology of sensory coding.* New York: Harper & Row.

Vattimo, G. (1988). *The end of modernity.* Baltimore, MD: Johns Hopkins University Press.

Wilson, A. N. (1992). *Jesus: A life.* New York: W. W. Norton.

Index

Note: A chapter reference, e.g. *Ch 2*, is given where a whole chapter is devoted to the subject in question. However, for most items, most references are given to specific pages or page sequences. The page numbers of especially important citations are often given in *italics*.

ISBN 0-275-95676-8

90000>

EAN

9 780275 956769

HARDCOVER BAR CODE